The Chronicles of Hernia

Award-winning comedy writer Barry Cryer was born in Leeds. He failed a B.A. in English Literature due to the outbreak of the Second World War (which had happened 16 years before but upset him greatly). One of our best-loved comedians, and a regular on 'I'm Sorry I Haven't A Clue', he has written for Britain's comedy giants, including Morecambe & Wise, Jasper Carrot, Tommy Cooper, Richard Pryor and Rory Bremner – to name but a few.

This book was previously published in 1998 as *You Won't Believe This But . . .*

D1147519

By the same author

Butterfly Brain

Pigs Can Fly

The Doings of Hamish and Dougal: You'll Have Had
Your Tea?
(Barry Cryer and Graeme Garden)

The Chronicles of Hernia

Foreword by Michael Palin

BARRY CRYER

Virgin BOOKS

First published as *You Won't Believe This But* . . . in Great Britain in 1998
by Virgin Books

This revised and updated edition first published in 2009 by
Virgin Books
Random House, 20 Vauxhall Bridge Road,
London SW1V 2SA

2 4 6 8 10 9 7 5 3 1

www.virginbooks.com
www.rbooks.co.uk

Addresses for companies within The Random House Group Limited can be found at:
www.randomhouse.co.uk/offices.htm

The Random House Group Limited Reg. No. 954009

A CIP catalogue record for this book
is available from the British Library

ISBN 9780753522158

The Random House Group Limited supports The Forest Stewardship
Council [FSC], the leading international forest certification organisation.
All our titles that are printed on Greenpeace-approved FSC-certified
paper carry the FSC logo. Our paper procurement policy can be found at
www.rbooks.co.uk/environment

Typeset by Palimpsest Book Production Limited,
Grangemouth, Stirlingshire
Printed and bound in Great Britain by
CPI Bookmarque Croydon, CRO 4TD

For Terry, Tony, Dave, Bob and Jacqui
(not forgetting Ruby, Evan, Tom, Archie,
Hope, Martha and Constance)

CONTENTS

Why I Like Barry Cryer
by Michael Palin   1
Prologue   5

1   Was That Where the Windmill Was?   13
2   Baubles, Bangles and Leeds   25
3   South as a Boarder   46
4   Six Times a Day   50
5   *Starlight Expresso*   54
6   A Little Night Music   63
7   The One Ronnie   68
8   Name Drops and Roses   72
9   Familiar Faces   77
10   A Packet of Players   80
   Never Mind What I Think, the
   Listeners Love Him
   by Humphrey Lyttelton   90
11   The Aural Dance   92
12   Willie Nilly   101
13   One Man's Mate is Another Man's Python   108
14   Ever Ev   112

15	The Price Is Right	120
16	On Your Marx	122
	Barry Cryer – An Appreciation	
	by David Nobbs	127
17	The Skin Game	128
18	Goon But Not Forgotten	130
19	The Good Companion	132
20	Max to the Wall	139
21	Ace King Jack	141
22	Two of a Kind	143
23	Frost in All Areas	147
24	Les Majesty	151
25	Welcome to Morecambe	155
26	Stand Up and Be Counted	160
27	My Favourite Martian	169
28	Get off! Sorry, I Don't Do Requests	176
	Please Accept This as an Invoice	
	From Colin Sell	181
29	Considered Trifles	182
30	This Is Your Desert Island	185
31	First Act	191
	Baz and His Filofags	
	by Graeme Garden	211
32	Afterthoughts	213
33	Under the Influence	230
	Acknowledgements	245

WHY I LIKE BARRY CRYER

By Michael Palin

THERE ARE MANY things I like about Barry Cryer and they all stem from one great quality. How I wish I could remember it. What I do remember is meeting Barry for the first time, and that's always a good thing – if you remember when you first met someone it shows that they've made a greater than average impression. For instance, I can remember exactly when I first met my wife. I was sixteen and she and Barry were walking hand in hand . . . No, no, sorry, sorry! That was someone else's wife. I first met Barry in 1966 at a Methodist hall in Crawford Street, which runs off Baker Street in London. I was unmarried, blond and fresh out of university, and suddenly I thought, What the hell, I'll become a Methodist. (We're talking about the sixties, remember!)

No, to be honest, I entered the Methodist hall, not because I wanted to become a Methodist but because I was un-married, a bit Japanese and fresh out of university and I had grown out of Dean Martin and Jerry Lewis. My new heroes were Marlon Brando and Monty Clift and all those Methodist actors who could make scratching the left ear as exciting as a whole afternoon at Bertram Mills.

No, the real story is that I went into the Methodist hall in Crawford Street because I wanted to be a comedy scriptwriter. It really was 1966, and I was friends with Terry Jones. We had written comedy material that caught the eye, ear, nose and throat of David (then Mr David) Frost, whose producer, Jimmy Gilbert, had asked us to come along to the first meeting of writers for a new series to be called *The Frost Report*.

I entered that Methodist hall with some trepidation. After all, the funniest writers in England were gathered upstairs (a fact that still could not prevent the long-term fall in numbers of Methodists) and I was a nobody, a new boy. For some reason Terry was unable to come along, and I had to climb the stairs unaided. I could hear the ripple of easy laughter and felt suddenly, sharply, terrifyingly unfunny.

I was on the point of apologising, making some excuse about having got the wrong Methodists and disappearing down the stairs, never to be a scriptwriter again, when a man with large distinctive glasses and very secure hair stepped forward and held out his hand.

'I'm Barry Cryer,' he said, which I thought was quite funny, but certainly not hysterical.

'I'm Michael Palin,' I blurted out, messing up the timing horribly.

'Come and meet some of the others,' he said. 'We're all new here.'

So Barry introduced me to the world of comedy in a Methodist hall on Crawford Street. He was like a boy you hope you'll meet on the first day of school, but rarely do.

We became friends – it's very hard not to with someone like Barry – and because he's such a decent man he was too polite to say 'Not in a million years!' when Terry and I asked him to help write and perform some sketches for a misbegotten enterprise called *Line-up Review*. This took place very late at night, without an audience, after a dreadfully serious arts programme, and on BBC2. However, we were so successful (how could they tell?) that we were promoted to a slot during or even before the dreadfully serious arts programme.

One night we recorded our little clutch of sketches (I remember Barry, dressed as a trainee Superman, having to jump off a chair very badly), then went off home to watch the programme go out an hour or so later. Our sketches were duly run to the usual icy studio silence, only this time there was a difference. Dennis Potter was the studio guest immediately following and it was clear that he was extremely agitated about something: Was it the state of *Play for Today*? Was it the government's attitude to censorship? Was it the financing of the BBC?

No. What had really got up the nose of Britain's leading television playwright was having to come all the way up from

Gloucestershire to appear in a television programme in which men dressed as Superman jumped off chairs. His outburst was virulent, full of indignation and outrage, but at least it was a reaction. And it made electrifying television. Next week we were dropped.

Barry, I think, is as proud of this moment as I am. My only regret is that it meant the end of our convivial writing sessions in the kitchen at Biddulph Mansions, where Barry's mother poured us cups of tea and treated Terry Jones and me as errant sons.

Barry remains the one you can't help making friends with and, although, as far as I know, he has never again pulled on the cloak and the saggy tights of a superhero, he has found other ways to make me laugh – more or less continuously – ever since.

Michael Palin, Gospel Oak, London, England, Europe, The Western Hemisphere, The World, The Solar System, etc.

PROLOGUE

ERIC IDLE AND I took a week's break years ago, in Tenerife. We began to frequent a bar run by a Liverpool couple. There we met a man who would, in days gone by, have been described as a 'remittance man'. There existed certain individuals who were not engaged in gainful employment, but received, usually on a monthly basis, regular payments which enabled them to pursue their lifestyle. Where these payments came from was shrouded in mystery – they were thus known merely as remittance men.

Anyway, the aforementioned man in the bar in Tenerife engaged us in conversation early on in our holiday. It transpired that he was a (very) frustrated writer and regarded us as kindred spirits. I'm always struck by the number of people who tell me they've always fancied being a writer and would have got round to it if only they'd had the time. They just assume they would have the talent. All went well until the end of the week, when our new friend suddenly launched into a tirade of abuse at Eric and I, describing us as 'sponges' who came into the bar merely to soak up as much character and atmosphere as we could, having no real interest in the people as such. This verbal attack was about to become physical when he was ejected.

I've never forgotten that and still get the odd twinge of guilt whenever I relate a story about a friend or colleague, as if I'm somehow sapping their lifeblood, drop by drop. But then I snap out of it because I know it's really born of a desire to share a funny or unusual incident with as many people as possible.

That was the first and possibly the last bit of self-analysis in this book. Emma, my former agent, whom Jane Austen would surely have written about had she known her, rebuked me, as I said, for concentrating throughout on other people and deftly removing myself from this saga. Whence this modesty/cunning? I have no idea, unless it's because I find other people more interesting than myself. I sometimes think I'm an empty vessel into which they pour themselves. Bill Franklyn, whom you will meet later in the book, called me 'the war correspondent'.

'You love it all,' he once said. 'The noise, the people, the sound and the fury and then you come away from the battle-field and tell us all about it.'

So maybe you should simply regard me as your very own cut-price Kate Adie.

Let me ease you gently into my maddening habit of digression, which you will come across with increasing frequency and possibly annoyance during the course of this narrative. I mentioned Jane Austen a few lines ago. One of my favourite cartoons depicts Miss Austen sitting in her publisher's office. *Pride and Prejudice* lies on his desk. He says to her, 'It's very good, Miss Austen, but all this effing and blinding will have to go.'

Another favourite shows a wine waiter displaying a bottle to a customer and saying, 'I think you'll find this an audacious little number, sir, and I can assure you it won't fuck up your hamburger and chips.'

See what I mean about digression? Talking of digression reminds me (!) that my partner on the Kenny Everett show, Ray Cameron, once said to me, 'I wish I could just once mention something that didn't remind you of something else.'

Speaking to you from my self-appointed psychiatrist's couch, I am well aware that the chronicle of my life emerges as a nonstop parade of fun, incidents and interesting people. All right, you be the judge of that, but that's how it has seemed to me. But, as with all of us, there's more to it than that. As a husband, father and writer, there have been traumas, depressions, dramas and disappointments aplenty. The responsibility of marriage changed me and, even after 47 years, I'm still not convinced that I passed the audition.

During my show-business career, I've been dumped from more than one TV series in favour of a younger, more talented performer. It hurts, but Ardal O'Hanlon and Tom O'Connor are still friends of mine.

Ours is a tough and competitive business and yet I seem to have spent years being with people I like and laughing a lot.

A man once said to me, 'What would be your ideal day?'

I said, 'Arriving to work with some people, having a cup of tea and a gossip, taking them to the bar at lunchtime, doing a bit of work in the afternoon, more tea and then further merriment in the evening. That's my ideal day.'

'I thought that's what you did anyway,' he said.

Now and again someone has lifted the lid of the cauldron and I've spotted some nefarious dealings and betrayals. But the lid seems to slam shut almost immediately. Escapism or realism? Once again, you be the judge.

Later on in the book, I refer to the scourge of eczema, which plagued me for years. The conviction that I had then, that show business and I were not destined to be a lasting partnership, depressed me for a long period. Make-up was painful to apply and I came to believe that the frenetic lifestyle didn't help either. But, thank God, the eczema and that misplaced conviction eventually passed.

Who was it that said 'Let something spoil your breakfast but never your lunch'? My sentiments exactly. Maybe eczema gave me a thick skin. That does not mean, however, that I'm not prone to bouts of affection, sympathy or anger. At a rehearsal, I once shouted furiously at Ronnie Corbett and walked out, slamming the door. I then burst into tears. He followed me out, concerned. Soon we were laughing.

I used to think I was always losing my temper at the wrong moment – but is there a wrong moment to lose your temper? For better or worse, anger should be genuine and not calculated.

As a comic turned writer, I always felt a bit of a fraud, a sort of fellow traveller in the company of my vocational, dedicated colleagues. Admittedly, I had some sort of half-baked idea of being a journalist when I embarked on my English Literature degree at Leeds University, but I think that was more of a justification for being there than a genuine ambition. After a job interview with the then editor of the *Yorkshire Post*, Sir Linton Andrews, I was swiftly disabused of going into the profession. He informed me, firmly but kindly, that he was looking for someone of around fifteen to make tea and learn the trade, or someone older who had lived a little and could bring some experience to bear. I fitted into neither category. I left his office somewhat stunned and returned to university intent on enjoying myself. Totally irresponsible, but it seemed a good idea at the time.

The next big let-down was my first year's results, but I'll deal with that later. It's been a roller coaster all the way, but roller coasters are meant to be fun, aren't they?

Like many people in our business, I am interviewed quite regularly. Here again the detached-observer syndrome comes into play, not that I'm trying to conceal anything, you understand, but they always ask the same questions – which are rarely of a probing nature: 'How did you start? Who's your favourite comedian? Are the new lot good? When did you first realise you were funny?'

Admittedly, that last one has always foxed me. Answer, 'At school when I had the classroom in a roar,' and you sound conceited; answer, 'I'm never sure that I am,' and they wonder what you're doing in the game anyway.

You go into automatic pilot and deliver the answers that you always give, like a litany. Mind you, an interviewer once asked me, 'Do you believe in God?' That woke me up.

Peter Sellers was once being interviewed on American TV and the host said, 'You've been described as the funniest man in England.'

Peter made modest noises.

'So go on, be funny,' said the host.

Peter stalled and then said, 'It's been said that you're the finest talk-show host in America.'

It was the host's turn to murmur humbly.

'I didn't say it,' added Peter.

There I go again, talking about other people. As it happens, I think Peter Sellers was hugely talented, so I mention him in an attack of taste.

I have been accused of sycophancy in my time and I plead guilty in so far as I can be effusive with people I admire, but never with people I don't, I assure you. I think you should thank anyone whose work or personal actions have given you pleasure and I make no apology for that.

I talk so much that it's been said my silence is deafening.

I have a face that, in repose, has a look of acute anxiety, leading people to ask me what's wrong. I then flash my rictus grin, which probably alarms them even more. An alluring picture, isn't it? Do you wonder that I prefer to dwell on other people? If that makes me sound like a performing flea, so be it. I'm just a practising catalyst. I like to bring out the best in people – if I can find it. If I can't, I pretend that I have.

There are times when you have to admit defeat. Dick Vosburgh and I once worked with a producer in whom it seemed impossible to find a redeeming feature. In the peace and quiet of the gents, Dick vented his spleen upon the unfortunate man in no uncertain terms. I noticed the ENGAGED sign on one of the doors. Who knew who was behind it? I signalled to Dick, who ceased his vituperation in mid-flow. 'And those are my sentiments,' he said, 'as sure as my name's Barry Cryer.'

Frank Muir called me a 'good old workhorse', while comedian Jimmy Edwards jovially (I think) always referred to me as 'the whore'. The truth, perhaps, lies somewhere in between.

When I wrote Danny La Rue's nightclub shows, I knew I was known as a 'blue' writer. The first time I met Denis Norden at Danny's club he shook me by the hand. 'I never knew there were so many cock jokes in the world,' he said.

Then I entered my clean phase and wrote searing social comment for David Frost. We were the smartarse alternatives of our day, I suppose.

Then came Kenny Everett and suddenly I was an innovative, imaginative writer, using the medium to the full. For Russ Abbott, I was a traditional sketch and gag writer. To sum up, I could claim to be a stand-up chameleon.

So what am I? Writer, comic, or a bit of both? I performed as chairman in old-time music hall and fronted *The Stand-up Show* on TV with new comedians. I'm not versatile, just confused. Maybe I think that if I'm a moving target I'll be harder to hit. If you're blamed for one thing, you can always imply that's not what you really do, it's just a sideline. But as Sylvester Stallone once said, through an interpreter, 'You can run, but you can't hide.' I'll keep running – at least until I've finished this book. Now you see me, now you don't. Mainly because people of my age tend to do radio.

I'm getting old, I tell you! As the great American comic Alan King said, 'I'm 62 and people call me middle-aged – how many 124-year-old men do you know?' Well, I was 62 when I wrote this, maybe 63 when the book was finished. I'm at the age when you look on your body as a place where anything that still works hurts. My back goes out more than I do. My shampoo is Tippex and Go. Allow an old man his jokes.

But *nil desperandum*! Do you realise that the oldest man in the world is *still alive*? [Breaks into chorus of 'I'm Still Here'.]

ONE

WAS THAT WHERE THE
WINDMILL WAS?

I KNEW HE was dead. He sat in the chair, quite still, with his glass in his hand. That has nothing to do with what follows, but it made you start reading, didn't it?

'Was that where the Windmill was?' We were in Great Windmill Street, off Piccadilly Circus in London. The question was posed by number two son as we walked in the midday sunshine. The Windmill, dear reader, if you are under fifty, was a small theatre, born in the thirties, that ran triumphantly during the Second World War (1939–1945) under the slogan 'WE NEVER CLOTHED'. This was an allusion to the fact that the show featured nudes. Young nudes, to boot. I always compared the show to an end-of-term concert at a girls' school gone mad.

'What is your connection with the Windmill?' you ask. A good question and one that will be answered.

In 1957 I had come down to London – 'down' in so far as I was born in Leeds – on an overnight train to St Pancras, with a seventeen-day return ticket. What I intended to achieve in seventeen days in London I'm not quite sure. But there I was.

I found digs in North Finchley, with a spiritual landlady. She entertained gentlemen at midnight. Mine was not to reason why; mine was but to sleep throughout. 'What is the connection with the Windmill?' you cry with mounting irritation.

On my sixteenth day in London, I had obtained an audition at the Windmill. These were legendary affairs which took place every Wednesday morning from about 10.30 a.m. A parade of would-be stars would turn up, step on the stage and sing, joke, eat fire or play an instrument until a ghostly voice from the darkness of the stalls would bark, 'Next.' The voice belonged to Vivian Van Damm, the owner, known to all as 'VD'.

The show featured – nay, was built on and around – nudes. The customers, most of whom were fully paid-up members of the faded-raincoat brigade, had not come to see the comedians. You were there on sufferance. They never heckled; the mood was not hostile, but one of patient silence. What a school. After that, whatever the circumstances, you weren't frightened of any audience, ever again.

I'll never forget the audition. It was a Wednesday and it was raining. I had rung the Windmill to ask for an audition. To my amazement, they agreed. I duly turned up with the clothes I stood up in and my sheet music. The music was 'Heartbreak Hotel', the current Elvis Presley hit.

A footnote here. In those days, you could buy the sheet music of hit songs enabling you to reproduce them as well you might on your piano, guitar or whatever came to hand or foot.

I told my jokes and then came the climax of my 'act' – an impression of Elvis at his army medical. This consisted of wrapping myself in a towel and emulating the tremulous Presley tones – the hilarious premise being that Elvis, trapped in a cold corridor, discovered his singing style. This blithely ignored the fact that Elvis was already a world star by the time he entered the army and would, therefore, have left it a bit late to discover his style at that stage.

I told my jokes and sang my song.

The voice in the darkness said, 'Do you know any more jokes?'

I did but I had no more music.

'Ronnie will busk,' said the voice.

Ronnie Bridges, the pianist who became a friend, duly did. I sang, yet again. I can't remember what.

Silence. Then, 'Would you like to work here?'

'Yes,' I said.

Silence. Apparently, I was about to become a Windmill comedian. When? Three weeks on Monday? Six months hence? Next year? A man appeared on the stage. His name was John Law and he also became a friend. He led me to dressing room 12a. I was on that afternoon.

I was shell-shocked. Someone loaned me some make-up. I smeared pancake on my face. The whole sensation was unreal. I hadn't even rung my mother in Leeds. There was no time.

The first show was at 12.15 p.m. and I was on early. I was the bottom-of-the-bill comic. I remember the thought crossing my mind: Who *had* been the bottom-of-the-bill comic until today? Or was I an addition to the bill? I later discovered that the latter was the case. If the old man liked your audition, you were in. Sometimes that very day, as I found out.

I was led down the stone steps and met the stage manager, Johnny Gale – a mountainous man whose trousers stopped just under his armpits. He smiled and I was on. The theatre was pretty full, even for that first show. The atmosphere was quiet, almost reverent. Two men, I recall, opened newspapers and began to read as I started my act. I could actually hear them breathe. They were alive. I ploughed on. I suddenly had an out-of-body experience. I looked down on myself, standing there in my street clothes, intoning a joke concerning my grandfather's habit of taking liver salts every day with the result that, after he died, we had to beat his liver to death with a stick. I know! I know! They didn't laugh either! Someone went to the gents. Would that I could have joined him.

Elvis sang in the cold corridor at his army medical. He finished. So did I. I walked off the glass stage to the sound of my own feet. I ascended the steps to dressing room 12a.

'Very good,' said John Law as he removed his trousers.

The magician on the bill was too busy tearing newspapers and forcing two doves into a hidden compartment in a table to even look up. I sat down.

The tannoy spoke: 'Barry Cryer to Mr Van Damm's office.'

I got up and made my way to the sanctum sanctorum.

The great man sat ensconced behind his desk. He greeted me – rather warmly, I thought. I was not invited to sit down. I stood, shifting from one foot to the other between the desk and the fish tank. The fish reminded me of the audience I had just left.

'Now,' he said.

He then proceeded to dissect my act, joke by joke, line by line, excising, adding, subtracting and transposing. Then, with a friendly nod, he dismissed me. I stumbled from his office and went upstairs for a shaky cup of tea.

It was an interesting phenomenon at the Windmill that you could be sacked for being in the wrong part of the building, i.e. the girls' dressing rooms, but you could sit and have a cup of tea with them in the canteen wearing only a flimsy robe and a G-string. Them, that is, not you. I sat alone at a table with my thoughts. I suddenly had a new act. I went through it again and again in my head. I got up and went down the steps to the stage door. I went out into the daylight in Archer Street. It was quiet. It usually was, except on Monday mornings when it was packed with musicians looking for work. A sort of open-air labour exchange. I walked on, into Berwick Street market.

It wasn't until a jovial cry of 'Hello, darling' assailed my ears that I remembered I hadn't taken my make-up off.

I was in a daze. I went back to the theatre and up to the dressing room. I sat.

Encouraging words came from my companions, even the magician. I was particularly moved by his words as he spent his whole day preparing for the next show. I never saw the man relax all the time we shared that dressing room. Before I knew it, I was called back on stage for the second show. In an even thicker haze than before, I did my revised act. Same reaction. Back to the dressing room. 'Barry Cryer to Mr Van Damm's office.' Same routine. Between the desk and the fish tank. The fish were going to get to know me quite well that day. Six shows. Five times I was summoned to the office. By the end of the day I had gone through about three new acts and my brain was awash with jokes and lines. Between the third and fourth shows I rang my mother: 'I'm a Windmill comedian.'

'Oh, yes,' she said.

How could I start explaining exactly what a Windmill comedian was? She seemed pleased and puzzled in equal proportions.

Stage, dressing rooms, office, canteen, walk, 'Hello, darling', dressing room, stage, pub . . .

It was nearly midnight. I sat, slumped. The ever friendly John Law and I had a drink. I had survived my first day. I *was* a Windmill comedian.

In my frenzied, robotic progress, I had failed to notice the brilliant top-of-the-bill comedian. His name was Bruce

Forsyth. Wearing a black suit, white shirt and tie, which I found very impressive, he did a routine of impressions, mimes and jokes which I was to watch each and every day from then on. He actually got some laughs from the seekers after culture who sat before us. I marvelled at him.

From appearing as a dancer with his wife, he had progressed to being a solo, stand-up comedian. In between stints at the Windmill, he appeared in summer shows at such venues as the Sparrow's Nest, Lowestoft, where he learnt his trade, cajoling, bullying, wheedling and charming his audiences, until they found themselves where they belonged: in the palm of his hand.

Outside the theatre were 'honours' boards, upon which, in gold lettering, you could read the names of the many distinguished alumni who had served their apprenticeship and then gone on to find fame elsewhere. Tony Hancock, Peter Sellers, Harry Secombe, Jimmy Edwards and many more. Bruce had yet to find his national fame but Mr Van Damm had put his name on the board while he was still working there – a singular honour. But disillusion was setting in. Bruce confided to me one day that he was thinking of packing it all in and opening a tobacconist's shop. The very next year, 1958, he did his first Sunday night at the London Palladium. I bumped into him in the street as he came from a press conference before his first show. I inquired about the tobacconist's. 'Postponed,' he said.

Between the fourth and fifth show on that first day, I had

a call to say there was someone at the stage door to see me. This only added to the unreality. Who knew I was there? There was only one way to find out. I went. Standing in the pouring rain in Archer Street was a man with shoulder-length hair and a floor-length overcoat. He had a pile of books under his arm. Suddenly I remembered him. He was my predecessor at the auditions that morning. It all seemed so long ago.

I had watched him getting ready as we waited beneath the stage for our turn. He had set up a box on a chair and then opened it. A light went on inside of it revealing a mirror in the lid. The box was full of make-up. He proceeded to daub his face with the most grotesque clownlike mask. He then donned what is known in the trade as a 'fright' wig, with the hair standing straight up. Then, as the strains of the current auditioner drifted down from above, he took out a loud checked jacket and a pair of baggy trousers from a holdall and put them on over his clothes. From yet another bag, he produced a music stand, a trombone and a rubber clarinet. He was ready.

He nodded at me and climbed the stairs to the stage. I followed him and stood in the wings to watch. He was called on. He set up the music stand and placed a wad of sheet music on it. He raised the trombone to his lips and oper-ated the slide. It came off in his hand. The music slid in a waterfall from the stand on to the floor. The stand fell over. He bent to pick it up, together with the music, and his trousers fell down. I assumed this was all part of the act. It was all hypothetical, anyway. 'Next!'

He never even got to the rubber clarinet. He gathered up his impedimenta and trudged off the stage. He smiled at me, shrugged his shoulders and descended the stairs. Now, he stood before me, his hair plastered by the rain and his coat dripping on the pavement.

'I heard you got the job,' he said. 'Congratulations.'

He shook my hand and walked off down Archer Street. I hadn't spoken. I don't think I could have done. The lump in my throat wouldn't have permitted it.

It was nearly midnight. I scurried along Shaftesbury Avenue and turned down into Lisle Street. There was a figure in every doorway. Why those ladies were known as 'brasses' I never did find out. Someone once told me it was short for 'brass nail' but I was none the wiser. They plied their trade from the gloom of the doorways, but it was a 'no sale' as far as I was concerned. Not from lack of inclination but funds. I hurried on to Leicester Square tube station to start my safari to North Finchley. Had today really happened? I climbed into bed. The hum of conversation from the kitchen drifted up the stairs. Mrs Catley was entertaining again. I fell into sleep and dreams of fish tanks, rubber clarinets and my grandfather taking liver salts.

I lasted seven months at the Mill, going from show to show. In case that sounds like smooth progress, let me explain. The old man had a sadistic streak. Towards the end of each show, he would inform you that he wanted to see a new act for the next show. You would then turn up at one of the Wednesday-morning auditions with all the first-timers and present your latest offering. As often as not, he would turn you down and you still didn't know if you would be working the next week. On one occasion, he auditioned me three times in one week, turning me down twice before finally accepting me on the Friday. 'Come on Sunday,' he said, which meant I was in the dress rehearsal for the new show and was still gainfully employed.

My time at the Mill was a period I will obviously never forget. My first job in London and a crash course in how to ply my trade. Not least, incidentally, the virgin from Leeds was deflowered. But that's another story.

Some time after I left, the Mill changed its policy to a mere five shows a day, which was regarded with some disdain by old hands like myself. Thirty-six shows a week was our routine and my pay packet reached the dizzy heights of £35. I always rather resented never breaking the pound-a-show barrier, but then again, to be earning that sort of money in 1957 gave little cause for complaint. Before I left, the old man gave me a letter which stated, 'I still think you're funny.' I will never forget his faith in me, the people I met and the sheer concentration of experience crammed into a few months.

There was never a place like it before and probably there never will be again. It died in the seventies, swamped by the tide of strip clubs, which purveyed something rather more explicit, due to the demise of the Lord Chamberlain's office, which had, up until then, censored all stage productions. One of their stipulations was that nudes were not allowed to move. After his Lordship's departure, they did little else. The Windmill died.

Over thirty years later, I set foot in the old building again. The stone steps were carpeted, the stalls had become a TV studio and the circle is now a bar. It's unrecognisable, but the memories flooded back.

In between shows, a loudspeaker announcement used to request patrons not to climb over the seats, to get nearer the front for the next show. This was usually drowned by the sound of men climbing over the seats to get nearer etc. This ritual was christened the 'Grand National' by Jimmy Edwards. There was a sign as you went in to the effect that artificial aids to vision are not permitted in this theatre. Anyone caught using same would be gently, but firmly, evicted by Big Peter, the house manager, who would grasp a collar and remove the owner without his feet touching the floor. Legend has it that a customer, having settled in his seat, put on a pair of binocular glasses, as advertised for 'enhanced vision at race meetings and sporting events'. Peter removed him and courteously bade him farewell in the foyer. The man, still wearing enhanced vision aids, set off down the stairs to the exit and, misjudging his footing, fell all the way down and broke his leg.

I remember Jimmy Edmundson, a comedian long forgotten now, who decided to enliven a dull afternoon by addressing the empty circle as if it were filled by a Russian trade delegation. This caused an unprecedented event. The stalls actually began to listen to what he was saying and some got up to look at the visitors. Jimmy then informed them that the Russians were lying down, exhausted after their long journey.

It's been a long journey from the Windmill to today, but you never forget the first time. My first engagement in London, I mean, not . . .

TWO

BAUBLES, BANGLES AND LEEDS

WHAT LED TO that journey to the Windmill? Bear with me, dear reader, as I lead you back to 1935. To 23 March to be precise. The early hours of the morning. A gusty, windy night, or so I'm informed – I was rather preoccupied at the time.

I was in no mood to appreciate that this was the day that Grimaldi, the great clown, died in 1788, and Sir Lumley 'Skiffey' Skeffington was born in 1771. Skiffey, you will of course remember, was the Prince Regent's fashion adviser. Chung Ling Soo, the magician, was killed on 23 March 1918 on stage at the Empire Theatre, Wood Green, in London, catching a bullet in his teeth. Joan Crawford was born on this day in 1904. Suddenly the pieces fall into place.

Back to the plot. Home was 12 Mount Pleasant Avenue, in the Harehills district of Leeds. 'Harehills' – what a sylvan image that conjures up. Nearby were 'Roundhay' and 'Sheepscar' – keep your illusions. Dad was an accountant.

Digression: An accountant was walking down the street and was confronted by a poor old tramp.

'Give us a quid,' said the tramp, 'I haven't eaten for three days.'

'Mmmm,' said the accountant, 'and how does this compare to the same period last year?'

Sorry about that – I was going to call this book *Butterfly Brain* and now you know why.

I enjoyed an uneventful, pleasant, middle-class childhood, until Dad died when I was still young. I was told he was ill, but it was left to a school 'friend' to break the news to me. To this day I miss him, though I wouldn't know his voice if I heard it on tape and there is no record of him at all, from those pre-video days. My only clues are two photographs. What was he like? Many years later, I did an after-dinner speech at Waddington's in Leeds. Waddington's are the makers of Monopoly, among many other activities. In the bar before dinner, a man approached me. He was retired, but still came in for a drink at the club. 'Are you Carl Cryer's son?' he asked. It was the first time I had ever met anybody, outside the immediate family, who knew my father. We talked for a mere ten minutes or so and a picture emerged of a friendly, well-liked man who . . . and then it was time to go in and sing for my supper. I never met that man again. The older I get, the more envious I am when someone mentions their father.

I remember golf trophies in the house and mysterious (to a child) visits from men who I later realised were Masons. My father was a Worshipful Master of his lodge and my wife and I found his effects after my mother died. The sash, the Bible, the apron. My father was a golfing, Masonic accountant. Anything further from me is hard to imagine. I sometimes look for the 666, the sign of the beast, on my scalp. I was the black sheep, and there was no show-business history whatsoever in our family. In fact, I had no such ambitions in that direction as a youngster, so it must be in the genes, somewhere far back.

My mother soldiered on, bringing up me and my brother John. It can't have been easy, even though she had the afore-mentioned Masonic help. Ever supportive, she always made sure there was a warm fire in the grate and a meal on the table. John was to leave, to join the merchant navy and then go to London to work for the Ministry of Agriculture and Fisheries, so I was brought up virtually as an only child.

My early school days evoke memories of Mr and Mrs Gannon in Talbot Road. She was an absolute virago and he was, well, let's just say, feeling no pain, as his florid face testified. Mrs Gannon would cane anybody who made a mistake playing the piano, right across the knuckles. It seems Dickensian now, but we were resilient and just assumed that life was like that. Years later, I saw the film *The Seventh Veil* and there was a scene in which James Mason smashed his cane down on Ann Todd's hands as she played the piano. My neighbours in the cinema must have wondered why I said 'Mrs Gannon' audibly.

I hold fond memories of our gang: John Andrews,

Dean Tasker, Dave Milligan and Alan Brown. I think we were all in love with Heather Rutherford, who lived further down the road. If you're reading this, Heather, thank you for activating my hormones. I remember walking in Potternewton Park and hearing of a keeper savaged by a red squirrel. You don't see them now. Maybe Potternewton was the Jurassic Park of its day. Minutes behind our house was Bracken Edge Football Ground, where we would watch Yorkshire Amateurs play. Their goalkeeper was Pieter Piechota, a Pole who had stayed in England after the war and married a local girl. The centre forward was Eddie Joyce, known to accept a cigarette from spectators on the touchline. Brylcreemed and Clark Gable moustached, he had a right foot like a cannon and a cough like the cannon going off.

At home our neighbours were, on one side, the Gills – Ernest became a vet in Edgware – and on the other, at number ten, the Patemans. Frank, the paterfamilias, was an eminence, chiropodist to the Princess Royal, no less.

Our gang used to have speedway races on the dell behind our house. Let me explain to the younger reader (there must be one). In the immediate post-war period of the late forties, dirt-track motor-cycle racing was enormously popular. On a Saturday night, we would travel on two buses and then up a hill, on an open-top tram, to Odsal Stadium in Bradford, to watch our heroes speed round the track. I made masks out of cardboard boxes, so that when the riders roared past, throwing up shale over the spectators, we remained standing. We decided to replicate this gladiatorial combat on the dell. Be not deceived by the name: it was waste ground. Another bucolic illusion. We stencilled club emblems on vests and threw ourselves round the track. The only time I saw a man killed was when Joe Abbott, a veteran of the Bradford team, overslid in front of me and was hit by a following rider. Due to my mask, I was still standing and saw the whole thing.

I also recall charity events in aid of Dr Barnado's Homes. I can still see my papier mâché collecting box, a little house with a slot in the roof for the money. We made a wishing well on the dell. It bubbled when you threw in a coin. This was to be achieved by Dave Milligan blowing into a garden hose buried in the ground. On the test run, this ran downhill and Dave was hauled out from behind the bush where he was hiding, suffering from a violent blowback of stagnant water. We also had a ghost train in our garage, with masks and skeletons leaping out of the dark as the customer was whirled round on chairs on castors.

The more observant among you will have noticed no mention of the Second World War. At my age, I thought it wise to specify the exact war, in case you didn't do your arithmetic earlier. The older readers must remember the war: it was in all the papers. The Patemans (see Princess Royal's chiropodist earlier) had an Anderson shelter in the garden. This was an underground shelter, named after a politician, as was the Morrison equivalent. This was indoors, usually a reinforced table, but the Anderson, ah . . . a veritable bunker. When the air-raid warning went (a siren, young reader), I would be plucked from my bed, zipped into my 'siren suit' (a precursor of the tracksuit, modelled on a garment favoured by Winston Churchill) and taken next door. Thence downwards to the shelter. I can still remember the smell of wet earth. How evocative smells can be. The aroma of rubber from my Mickey Mouse gas mask haunts me still. Have you noticed a mask motif creeping into the narrative? Something symbolic there, I feel.

The kettle would be put on in the shelter and we would play games and sing songs. Leeds was not really affected by the bombing raids, in spite of the fact that Barnbow, the Allies' main tank-producing plant, was just outside the city. The only direct hits, as I remember, were on the gallery and a pub, the Golden Cock. Hardly wide ranging, but, you must admit, representative. The port of Hull was flattened and we counted ourselves lucky. One night, Pat, one of the two Pateman daughters, carried me up the wooden steps after the all-clear had gone. Too early, as it transpired, and we heard the sound of a German bomber overhead. We looked up and there it was – a Dornier, I think. I can still remember the crosses on the wings. Around the same time my wife was a schoolgirl in Brighton, and recalls German planes unloading a spare stick of bombs as they flew home over the coast. Not to mention machine-gunning civilians as a diversion.

We had a London evacuee billeted on us and, sad to say, all I recall of our relationship was constant fights. He had been torn from his home, sent to the North, and was living in a completely alien environment. No wonder he was unhappy. I'd like to meet him again, shake his hand and challenge him to a game of conkers.

VE Day. As a ten-year-old war veteran, I could feel the vast sense of relief. Later, I would see Winston Churchill when he visited Leeds. Even then, I was reminded that my mother was a Victorian, born in 1896, and would have been able to see Queen Victoria had she ventured North. My father had been in the First World War, in the artillery, the Death and Glory Boys, and for years I had his skull and crossbones cap badge. As I write this, many years later, it's amazing to realise the time span in one family's life story. Another digression.

When I was quite young, I met an old man who had worked at the old Leeds theatres, the Hippodrome and the City Varieties, when he was a boy. He told me about the Fred Karno company visiting the town. Karno was a legendary theatre impresario, whose companies toured in comedy shows in the early part of the century. My new friend told me about the principal comedian in the show who was brilliant, handsome, conceited and loathed by the company. He was often 'off' due to loss of voice – a supreme irony when one considers how he was to become the biggest star in the silent films. His name was Charlie Chaplin. His understudy, on the other hand, was arguably as talented, but modest and liked by everybody. His name was Arthur Jefferson, to become slightly better known as Stan Laurel. If only I'd had a tape recorder to preserve the old man's memories.

But back to *this* old man's memories. Where were we? Ah yes, the end of the war. In 1947, I gained a scholarship to Leeds Grammar School. Had I but known, at precisely the same time, young Alan Bennett was arriving at Leeds Modern School, but we didn't meet until much later, in London. Yet another digression. I was told that a couple at a dinner party said they had been to the National Theatre the night before to see *The Madness of George III* (its original title). Someone on the other side of them turned and asked, 'What was that about Thora Hird?' I related this to Alan, who sent me one of his immaculately written postcards: 'Rehearsals have just commenced for *The Madness of Thora Hird*. The curtain rises to the clash of zimmer frames.' End of digression.

Leeds Grammar School. I was hit by a car as I was crossing the road to school on the first day. I landed on the bonnet and then on my feet in the road. The story of my life, so far (touches wood and clasps St Christopher keyring). The Grammar School buildings seemed huge. When I spoke there, years later, they all seemed smaller. What can it all mean? I soon fell into the role of a Bilko *manqué*. I was involved in the selling of black-market dinner tickets –

something I share with Frank Skinner apparently. This led to a visit to the headmaster's study and 'six of the best'. Why being hit with a cane should be so described has always puzzled me. To those who state, 'I was beaten at school and it never did me any harm,' I am tempted to reply, 'We'll be the judges of that.'

I sold the short cut for the cross-country run in a sealed envelope for two pence. I was undercut by another boy who had several and sold them for a penny. An early lesson in market forces. Always a corner cutter by instinct, I would write essays culled from reference books with deft application of cross reference. Once it went awry. One teacher, HK Black, known to his intimates as Hugh, sadistically read out to the class an essay I had 'written' on *Henry IV*: 'The narrative grips,' he said, 'but turn the page and lo! we have changed kings! behold – Henry V.' My last form master, PH Kelsey, who laboured under the soubriquet 'Pip', wrote on my report: 'He must learn that glibness is no substitute for knowledge.' Have I ever learnt!

Talking of *Henry IV*, I played Falstaff and shared the acting cup with my friend John Gledhill. This fell apart when presented to us by the then Princess Royal (see Pateman, F, chiropodist earlier). I took the cup and gave the base to John, getting my first laugh from an audience. The seeds were sown.

Memories of school friends – Harry Ognall became a judge, Richard Price the head of a company selling television programmes worldwide. Onward, onward.

I won an exhibition (sub-scholarship) to Leeds University, my supportive mother behind me all the way. New friends: Jimmy Simmons, poet and singer, capable of playing his guitar and singing while standing on his head, later to become famous in his native Ireland; Wole Soyinka, who sang Tom Lehrer songs, became a hero in the Nigerian civil war and later won the Nobel Peace Prize; Tony Harrison, National Theatre glories yet to come, being forced into a dinner jacket and having Brylcreem forcibly rubbed into his hair before opening in the Rag Revue at the Empire Theatre. Little did I realise what a part that theatre would play in my life soon after.

Singing in the town hall with the university jazz band and being hit by flying pennies thrown by the charitable crowd. Girls, booze, bands, shows, total irresponsibility. Nemesis was on the premises. Fate lurked in the wings.

But it was a happy whirl, marred only by the fact that I fell in love. We got 'engaged' and then, at my birthday party, she informed me she was gay. We didn't say 'gay' then; I think she used the euphemism 'lesbian'. I was distraught. I left the house and was later found wandering the streets of Leeds in the early hours. We remained friends and had a reunion years later where she confirmed her lifestyle and told me she had been round the world. I was delighted. If you're reading this, Shann, all my love.

Although I had no show-business ambitions at the time, we all wrote, sang and performed in university shows and concerts. It was during this period that I first met an idol, Humphrey Lyttelton, who came with his band to the university union and the town hall. We always remained friends and he contributed to this book. Digression. Shall we have a digression symbol from now on? I suggest*. May we proceed? Where was I?

Oh yes, shows at university. Due to producer Jeff Smith falling off his motorbike – I think he stopped at the lights and forgot he hadn't got his sidecar with him – I was drafted in as producer of the Rag Revue (see earlier). Heady stuff – Brenda Bear (she had the voice of a lark and is now a postmistress in Suffolk), Wole Soyinka and I being embraced by the Lord Mayor, Alderman Beevers, in front of the audience. 'If only the whole world could be like this,' he opined, 'black and white.' How true, how true.

Wilfred Pickles, a radio legend, opened our week of charity, insisting he would do it for nothing but presenting an expenses bill that forced us to ask the university hierarchy to bale us out. Wilfred, a man of rare gifts – in every sense – would pay for rounds of drinks with a cheque. On it was a cartoon of himself and, of course, his signature. They were rarely cashed, but framed and put up behind the bar. I rest my case.

The university was nearly divided down the middle by the imaginatively named University Road. The social area was on one side and the academic premises on the other. The consensus of opinion was that I rarely crossed the road.

Retribution was at hand. My first-year results appeared. To say that I was shocked would be a lie. I'd been expecting them. Out into the cruel world: opening crates in the basement of Lewis's department store; working in the office of a TV shop – that lasted one day, but I had a wonderful leaving party. And then Leeds Highways Department as a clerk. This was a happy period with Harry Blackwell and the gang. I remember chasing a colleague with one of the old, heavy rulers and jumping out from behind shelves to strike a visiting councillor across his waistcoat by mistake. How I didn't get the sack I'll never know. Visits to the pub – a night in the exotically spelt Fforde Grene in Harehills, getting home, the bedroom going round and round. Never again, never again. I believe those words to be so true that I'm still using them.

Tom O'Connor once observed that, after a few pints, everywhere in a pub seems downhill. How true.

It was during this period that I was asked to produce the following year's Rag Revue. Back in the old routine with student friends who had, unlike me, survived the first year. An agent came up to Leeds from London to see someone – not me, I hasten to add – saw my act in the show and offered me work. What had I to lose? Stanley and Michael Joseph, the brothers who ran the City Varieties Theatre, offered me a week's work. After prancing around on the stage of the Empire in front of family and friends for charity, beginning to think I was good, this was like a douche of cold water.

My first professional engagement. The veteran comic on the bill gave me a glowing introduction and I entered to the sound of my own feet. It was a sunny afternoon and I counted eighteen people in the audience, most wearing raincoats. We used to call them commercial travellers, the sales reps of their day. Some twelve minutes later, I left the stage, also to the sound of my own feet.

I learnt the lesson, before my Windmill days, that the audience had come to see strippers, not some raw young comedian.

During my week at the Varieties, I was living at home. I realised that the possibility of my mother, a decent middle-class woman, ever coming to see me at that den of iniquity was remote. The audience, as I've indicated, was usually male and, whatever weather, raincoated. It was a no-go area. However, I clung to the thought that she might . . .

Monday, Tuesday and Wednesday came and went. I came home every night, ate my supper and went to bed. She never asked how the show had gone, never mentioned where I'd been. I gave up. On the Saturday, I arrived at the theatre for the matinée. The imposing woman in the box office beckoned me over and asked, 'Was that your mother last night?'

'Was what my mother last night?' I replied.

She explained. The box office is in a small alley off the Headrow in Leeds. She had spotted a small woman in a headscarf (very uncharacteristic of my mother, and it must have been an attempted disguise) hovering uneasily. Finally she came up to the window.

'What time's Barry Cryer on?' she asked.

She was informed I would be appearing in about five minutes. Could she buy a ticket? No, she could go in.

'I somehow knew it was your mother,' said the woman at the box office.

My mother was taken in by a commissionaire and shown to a seat, or, rather, shown a seat, as she declined to sit, but opted to stand at the back. A stripper was just finishing her act. My mind boggles at my mother's reaction. Then I came on, did my act, and she fled into the night. Later, we had our meal as usual and cleared the table. (Quite a jump. Sorry, sorry.)

As my mother was leaving the room she turned and said, 'That suit looked nice.'

Those four words said it all. She had been to see the show. Despite probing, I couldn't elicit any further comment from her. It was enough that she had been, and I was touched.

I went on the road in Variety, as it was known, appearing in theatres known as the 'Number Threes'. I knew what the 'Number Ones' were: the Palladium in London, the Empire Theatres in the big towns and the like, but I was always puzzled as to what 'Number Twos' were. No matter. I was definitely Number Three material. I was in shows rejoicing in titles such as *Nudes of the World*, *Strip, Strip Hooray* and *We've Nothing on Tonight*. It was a learning process. I fell in love again. This time with a beautiful stripper, sorry, exotic artiste. Her name was Charlotte. She asked me to read the commentary for her act. 'Now Desiree takes us to Paris,' I would intone as a cardboard Eiffel Tower was set up. For this, she paid me twenty Players on a Saturday night. But, as I say, I was in love. Then I realised she was more interested in the girls in the show. Lightning had struck twice. What was this fatal gift I had?

Two memories of the Royalty Theatre, Chester. I was, by now, labouring under the sad delusion that I was Terry Thomas. (My headmaster at Leeds Grammar School was called Terry Thomas. Strange, but true.)

Clad in a grey suit, pearl-hued waistcoat and sporting a carnation and a cigarette holder, I was apparently unaware that my Leeds accent rather marred the image. The stage manager saw my suit hanging in the dressing room the day I arrived.

'Is that carnation fireproof?' he asked.

I was bewildered.

Then he took a cigarette lighter and ignited the offending (plastic) flower. It flared up and the resultant burn ruined the lapel. I scoured Chester for what we used to call an 'invisible mender'. The lapel was restored. My relationship with the stage manager now had all the warmth of a fridge door opening.

One night between the shows (we did two a night), some other acts on the bill, including, I remember, Morgan

'Thunderclap' Jones, Wales's answer to Jerry Lee Lewis (what was the question?), invited me to join them in the circle bar. I was now a true professional. It was a hot summer night and I remember having four Merrydown ciders. I thought it was some sort of soft drink. I was so thrilled to be accepted by the others that I wasn't counting.

When I tried to rise from my seat, my legs remained locked. I was helped to an upright position. If the others felt concern, they concealed it. I went back to my dressing room and donned my suit. I went on the stage in a rosy glow, awash with hubris. My final joke, before the obligatory sentimental song with which I finished my act, was one I had borrowed from Max Miller. It never failed to get a laugh. It did that night. I sang my song and left the stage to a wave of silence. I commented to my friend, the carnation arsonist, that the joke had never let me down before.

He smirked. 'It may have something to do with the fact that you told it twice,' he said with relish.

Another lesson learnt. Well, no more Merrydown, anyway.

In the Regent, Rotherham, a notice at the side of the stage said: 'JOKES ABOUT THE SIZE OF THE AUDIENCE ARE NOT APPRECIATED AT THIS THEATRE'. I was gradually getting slightly better, learning the trade.

The Alexandra Gardens, Weymouth, where I worked with Norman Evans, a wonderful Lancashire comedian renowned for his 'Over the Garden Wall' sketch as a gossipy woman, reincarnated later by Les Dawson. Norman introduced me to Consulate cigarettes and his wife, who cooked sausages in the dressing room. Norman was not a well man and had to have a dressing room near the stage. I still remember the irony of the aroma of our menthol cigarettes mixed with the fragrance of sizzling sausages, beneath a large NO SMOKING sign. The theatre was constructed entirely of wood. In these days of non-smoking premises, it's strange to recall a pall of smoke that used to hang in every pub and, indeed, in theatres. You could see it floating towards you as you stood on the stage. When did you last see anyone smoking on television? Apart from Peter Cook, that is. I remember a commercial in the early days of ITV. The picture was of a beautiful woman smoking a cigarette. The caption read: 'ONLY A CAMEL CAN SATISFY ME'. Another age.

My baptism in show business proved short-lived. After some weeks on the road, I was out of work again. What to do? I crept back to Leeds with my tail between my legs. An instinct led me back to the Empire Theatre, where I asked to see Johnny Gunn, the stage manager, who had been a tower of strength with the student shows. He offered me a job as a stagehand, combined with a morning job emptying three bars, the stalls, circles and gallery, and then restocking and returning at night.

The stars came and went. I took every opportunity to watch them at the Monday-morning music rehearsal – the band call. The protocol was first come, first served. The top of the bill had no priority: the first act to put their music on the stage rehearsed first. Jimmy James, who, to me, epitomised music hall with his stooges (including, at one time, a young Roy Castle), arrived in Leeds and made sure he got his music down first before the top of the bill, Petula Clark. Petula was just starting a career as a singer, after appearing as a child actress in films. She had a current hit record, 'The Little Shoemaker' or something similar, and this seemed to irritate the great James, who had been a star comedian for years but now found himself 'second top', i.e. supporting singers he claimed never to have heard of.

The innocent and delightful Petula was totally unaware of this. She stood on the side of the stage watching Jimmy James and company rehearse with the orchestra. What she didn't know was that Jimmy had already spoken to the musical director and asked the band to busk 'The Little Shoemaker'. He and his colleagues duly and atrociously sang it, watched by a stunned Petula, who was obviously going to sing it in her act.

When she recovered, she tentatively approached Jimmy and informed him of this. He quietly and with great dignity told her that the song had been in their repertoire for some time. He kept this going for an hour or so, before letting her off the hook.

This sadistic tendency, even in the best of comedians, is an interesting one, implying their endless fight for survival. What Jimmy did to Petula was initially funny, but underlying it was a firm conviction that he should be top of the bill, not her.

Roy Castle told me that he appeared at the Prince of Wales Theatre in London with Jimmy and, yet again, the bill was topped by a singer, Slim Whitman, a country and western star of the day. Every night the audience was full of Slim Whitman fans and the aggrieved James found himself struggling with a young audience who had no idea who he was. He decided not to cut his act, but to speed it up. The original seventeen minutes were reduced to ten. He and his cohorts clattered down the corridor after coming off the stage and the star-dressing-room door flew open. There stood Slim Whitman, in Y-fronts, or the western equivalent.

'What's going on?' he asked Jimmy.

'You are,' was the reply, and Jimmy walked away.

The band had to fill in.

As my old friend Spike Mullins, who wrote 'Ronnie Corbett in the Chair' and other miniature masterpieces, once said: 'Never turn your back on a fully grown comic.'

One Monday morning, the five Smith Brothers, a Geordie close-harmony act, were rehearsing their act down on the stage. I say 'down' because I was, by now, working up in the fly gallery. This involved pulling on the lines (ropes) to raise and lower the cloths (scenery). The three lines were attached to a wooden batten on the top of the cloth. These were knotted round a cleat when the cloth was in place. As the brothers rehearsed below, I suddenly noticed the line unravelling and moving upwards. Realising that, if the cloth descended at speed, it could injure those on stage, your hero leapt forward and grabbed the lines. I went up with them. One of the other flymen grabbed me and the others waded in. The crisis was averted, but I had severe rope burns on both palms. I was taken to casualty at Leeds General Infirmary, where creams and bandages were applied.

I had managed to acquire an engagement (theatrespeak for 'get a job'), at the Theatre Royal, Bilston, and had been given the following week off work at the Empire. I set off, with mummified hands, struggling with my luggage. After a safari, involving changing trains at Birmingham, I arrived in Bilston on the Sunday. I checked in at a small hotel.

Walking through the town past the theatre, I heard the strains of music. I went in, as much out of curiosity as anything else. They were having a band call. I was later informed that they did this as the musicians would be down the pit (mining, not orchestral) the following morning. As I ran out, the hotel manager informed me that, if he had known I was appearing at the theatre, he would never have taken me in. Life was sweet.

I rehearsed and commenced a week of performing with my hands in my pockets. I got to the Wednesday and the manager rebuked me for my sloppy, hands-in-pockets demeanour. Appearing on the bill was a fire-eater, Bert Purches, brother of Danny, a gypsy singer. (Are you following the plot?) He saw my bandaged hands and inquired as to the problem. When I told him, he produced a large dock leaf and an evil-smelling potion in a bottle. He instructed me to smear the potion on my palms, place the dock leaf between them and sleep with my hands clasped together. Within 24 hours, my hands had healed. Ancient Romany remedy. Bert, I thank you.

When I was first booked for Bilston, a man rang me and asked, 'What's your billing matter?'

'What does it matter indeed!' I quipped, but he explained that 'billing matter' was the slogan beneath your name on the posters, a catch phrase or description. I told him I didn't have one.

'Make up one,' he commanded.

Bearing in mind my Yorkshire birth, I improvised. 'It snows tha knows,' I said.

The posters at Bilston duly announced: 'BRIAN CRYAN – BRITAIN'S NEWEST AND FUNNIEST COMEDIAN – IT SNOWS THA KNOWS'. I felt more alienated than ever.

THREE

SOUTH AS A BOARDER

DAVID NIXON, THE magician, was a big star on television by the fifties, appearing on *What's My Line?* and also in his own show. He was due to appear at the Empire in pantomime. He drove up to Leeds on the A1 – premotorway days – and his then wife, Paula, who was also appearing in the pantomime, took the same route in another car.

Unbeknown to him, she suffered a heart attack at the wheel and crashed off the road. David arrived in Leeds and was told the news. He collapsed and a doctor was sent for. After some discussion, which must have been painful for him, he typically announced that he was going on with the show. A replacement Prince Charming was sent for from London and rehearsals went ahead.

I was summoned to the office of the manager, Leo Lion (I swear that was his name). He was a dapper man with a military bearing and an ever-present carnation. 'Do you want to look after Mr Nixon?' he asked. I was puzzled as to why I had been singled out for this job. Due to my university adventures, I was regarded as something of an eccentric by the rest of the crew and rejoiced under the nickname of 'Toff'. Whether this had any bearing on the manager's decision, I will never know.

'Yes,' I replied, and thus began a friendship with David Nixon that lasted until his untimely death.

He was a delightful man, arrogant in his humility, and he had brought self-effacement to a fine art. 'I'm not the best magician in the country,' he once said to me, 'but I'm Charlie Charm.' He had an instinctive rapport with children which made him the perfect Buttons. (The more observant among you will have deduced that the pantomime was *Cinderella*. You have won a glass slipper and a ticket to the Spice Girls Ball.)

David played the part throughout, wearing a bellboy's hat. He was bald and said he didn't want to frighten the children. My job was to act as his dresser and prepare his tricks. Nothing can erase the memory of loading Bill and Ben and the two rabbits into a secret compartment in a table. Apart from that, the job was a joy.

Between the matinée and the evening performance, David would take a nap in his dressing room and I stood guard at the door. One day, round the corner from the stage door, came a figure I immediately recognised. Lord, then plain Bernard Delfont, was a major figure in show business and a member of the legendary Grade family, who had moved on from being agents to controlling theatres and TV stations.

'Is Mr Nixon in?' he inquired.

'Yes, he is,' I quavered, 'but he mustn't be disturbed.'

A pause.

'Good lad,' he said, and left.

I remember wondering whether my career was still-born at that moment, but I hadn't reckoned with the stature of the man, who acknowledged that I was only doing my job.

The panto continued after its tragic start and my friendship with David grew. He asked me about my ambitions, hopes, fears, love life and related topics, and told me I must get down to London. There was no YTV in Leeds in those days and Granada had only just started up in Manchester and, anyway, the theatre was my Holy Grail. I promised him I would hie me to London as soon as the panto finished.

David was a pioneer of magic on television and his shows were transmitted live, a formidable challenge for any conjurer. One of his tricks – sorry, illusions (I don't want to be drummed out of the magic circle; not that I ever was drummed *in*, but that's neither here nor there, as the man said when he put his truss on upside down) – consisted of presenting a packet of sausages to a member of the audience and asking them to select one, as if they were a pack of cards. He would then ask them to write their name on the sausage with a ballpoint pen. On this particular occasion, the man's name was Robert. He duly inscribed his name on the sausage.

There then took place much conversation and distraction, during which time David would be surreptitiously inscribing the name on another sausage by means of a pencil lead inserted under his fingernail. The original sausage (are you still following the plot?) would be destroyed by fire, as I remember, and in a welter of activity a sausage would be caught by a fork. The protagonist would be asked to remove it and read the name thereon. Of course, it was theirs. Applause and cries of 'Unbelievable'.

But this time, when David asked the man what he had written, he replied, 'Bob.' David said he had never got somebody back into the audience so quickly in his life.

FOUR

SIX TIMES A DAY

When the panto ended, I took David at his word. I said farewell to my mother and boarded a night train from Leeds to London. I had been given the address of a Mrs Catley in North Finchley and, having arrived, stiff-limbed, at St Pancras, I made my way, by tube, to my new home.

A word about Mrs Catley. She was, as it transpired, of a spiritualist persuasion and men were known to visit the house at all hours. I say 'men' for the very good reason that I never saw any women visitors. I refrain from further comment. I'm sure seances can be conducted at any time and spirits have no licensing hours. Our relationship was cool, but not unfriendly, although she did once say, after I had returned at dawn from a party, that it was like 'living with a volcano'. I had never seen myself in this lava-strewn role, but I was quite flattered.

This was during my Windmill period, previously described, and every night I would scurry down Lisle Street in Soho, after doing my six shows that day, and catch the northbound train to Finchley. In practically every doorway was its professional occupant, one of the aforementioned 'brasses'. 'Hello, dear' was the constant greeting as I shot past but, although I certainly had the inclination, I didn't have the remuneration, so I hurried on. After a week or two of this, my new friends got the picture and gave me a warm 'Good night'.

While on the subject of sex, which at the time was a purely hypothetical area to me, I should deliver the bombshell that I was deflowered at the Windmill. I had arrived, an angry virgin from Leeds, with a chip on my shoulder and an ache in my trousers. Ache and chips – a painful combination. Vivian Van Damm's assistant was a beautiful former Windmill girl, whom I shall call *** (with a hyphen). She was so beautiful that my heart, among other organs, leapt at the sight of her. There were two companies, 'A' and 'B', who alternated at the Mill and *** would do her rounds with a clipboard checking that everyone knew when they were on.

The comics, including myself, appeared in every show, so she didn't have to check with us, more's the pity. Between shows I would often – all right, always – pop over to the pub in Great Windmill Street for a swift application of inspirational lubrication. Returning one afternoon, I donned my trusty blue suit and made my way, beneath the stage, to the other side, from where I was to make my next entrance, to confront the customary silence of the audience.

*** was there, chatting to some of the girls. As I passed, I kissed her, full on the lips. Call it impulse, call it madness, or just call it wonderful. I continued on to garner my usual two titters at the performance. Later, upstairs in the canteen, we met.

'That was nice,' she said.

'What was?' I wittily riposted.

She apparently meant the kiss. As Willie Rushton used to say, my corduroys were in uproar. One thing led to another, over a period of days, and she broached the idea of spending a night together. I was stunned, and terrified.

The night was not to be at a hotel or her place, but at the flat of two of her friends, in a very fashionable part of London. I'm being deliberately vague about details, as I am a gentleman. And as you know a gentleman is someone who can play the accordion, but doesn't. That's the clean version anyway.

We duly made our way to the flat and I realised, to my alarm, that her friends were in residence and the four of us were to comprise a dinner party. Funnily enough, I don't remember the food at all. After some stilted conversation, we started to disperse to our rooms. Suddenly, my host took me to one side.

'Do you mind if I watch?' he said. 'I won't be any trouble.'

Not only was it going to be my first time, but a spectator sport. I somehow dissuaded him and repaired to the bedroom. I will draw a veil over that night. Suffice it to say, I would wish any man's inception to be as glorious and, indeed, any woman's. What * * * thought, I cannot say. She was still recovering from the shock of discovering that I had never done 'it' before. She later, much later, met my wife and, in the bonding way women seem to have, that no man will ever understand, they have been friends ever since.

A footnote: The morning after, our host, the would-be voyeur, entered the room, bearing a tray, on which was a full breakfast and the morning papers. He looked at * * *. 'Does he read as well?' he asked.

In conclusion: * * *, XXX. (Geddit?)

FIVE

STARLIGHT EXPRESSO

MY TIME AT the Windmill was drawing to a close, had I but known it. My boss, Vivian Van Damm, was a patriarchal, caring but slightly sadistic employer. Let me explain. Once a show was off and running, he would demand to see a new act if you wanted to be in the next show and remain in employment. One week I showed him my latest offering and he turned it down; but he asked me to come in the next day with a different one. This I had to devise while performing the six shows in the current opus. Somehow I managed, but this, too, was rejected. I was desperate. I asked if I could show him a third one on the Friday, the penultimate day of the show. He agreed. I duly turned up and did it for him. 'Come on Sunday,' was all he said, meaning the dress rehearsal for the new show. I was back in.

I had been at the Mill for seven months, six shows a day, six days a week, and was feeling rather complacent. There then occurred what I call the smack-on-the-back-of-the-neck syndrome. You're gazing ahead at the future, assuming you've got your life sorted, and ... whack. You wheel round, wondering what hit you. Something totally unexpected, that's what.

I was summoned to his office. 'You've been here long enough,' he said. 'Time for you to go into the cruel world.'

That was it. My short career as a Windmill comedian was over. As I said, he followed this up with a letter which simply said: 'I still think you're funny.' I treasured it for years and then lost it when we moved house.

Once again, I entered the highly overrated world of unemployment, signing on at what we used to call the Labour Exchange in Lisson Grove and trailing round agents' offices and going to auditions.

I got one for a show called *Expresso Bongo*, deliberately spelt with an X as it was assumed no one could spell 'espresso'. Which reminds me of the probably apocryphal story that *My Fair Lady* was originally meant as a play on words – an American idea of how a cockney would pronounce 'Mayfair'. Shades of Dick Van Dyke in *Mary Poppins*. Alan Jay Lerner, whom I knew (really? Oh yes), told me he was furious that he had written the song called 'On the Street Where We Live'. As a devoted Anglophile he realised, too late, that an Englishman of that period would have said 'in' not 'on', but, as the song was known round the world by then, there was nothing he could do about it. Interesting that a great lyric-ist would probably be the only person to be annoyed by one of his own lyrics. What a great story. Back to *Expresso Bongo*.

What to sing at the audition? How to get noticed, during the long day, when the auditioners would be seeing and hearing so many people? I sat in my room in North Finchley, hearing faint spiritualist noises from below, as Mrs Catley entertained her fellow media. Suddenly I had a revelation, as t'were St Paul on the road to Domestos: I would sing a song entitled 'Expresso Bongo'! Brilliant! Snag: it didn't exist. Solution: write one. So I penned an appropriate lyric. Next: music. I couldn't fill out a stave to save my life and Mrs Crotchet and I were strangers. Second revelation! Accompany self on bongos! Snag: can't play bongos. The following day, I went to Doc Hunt's, an emporium in Archer Street, near the Windmill stage door; fate was drawing me inexorably back. I met Doc Hunt himself.

'I want to hire some bongos,' I said.

He was amused. 'You what?' he asked.

'Hire some bongos!' I replied.

Bongo hiring was obviously not one of his major earners. 'How long for?' he wanted to know.

'Er . . . about two hours,' I replied.

A pause.

'Five guineas,' he demanded. (Another period note: one guinea equalled one pound, one shilling in old money. Most transactions seemed to be in guineas then.) I had seven pounds in my pocket.

I gulped. 'All right,' I said, and made my way to the Saville Theatre – now a cinema – opposite which was a café. The proprietor's son was, and is, Cat Stevens, as he was then. Please concentrate – I'll be asking questions later.

My name was called. It was, and is, Barry Cryer, for the record. I had been practising the bongos, loudly and abysmally, in the gents. I walked on to the stage. In the darkness were Wolf Mankowitz, the author of the book, and Monty Norman, the composer, later to write the *Bond* theme, both of whom later became friends.

'What are you going to sing?' they asked.

'Expresso Bongo,' I replied.

'Yes, that's right. What are you going to sing?' they asked again.

'A song called "Expresso Bongo",' I said.

Silence.

'OK,' came a rather puzzled reply.

I commenced hammering on the bongos, which threatened to fall from between my legs. I sang or rather shouted my saga of 'A kid from the backstreet – with a new beat'. I'm glad you weren't there.

I finished with a final roll on the bongos, which promptly fell to the floor. More silence. And more. I could hear a muffled conversation from the darkness. Monty Norman appeared on the stage.

'Thank you, Barry. Where did you get that song?' he said.

'I wrote it last night,' I replied.

His relief was overwhelming. 'Really?' he asked.

I later realised they had been horrified to discover there

was a song called 'Expresso Bongo' and that they might have
been sued. I think it was their relief and possible amusement
at my chutzpah that got me the job. ('Chutzpah' means sheer
gall and is not a character in Henry IV.)

Bongo ran for some ten months. We luckily opened just
ahead of *West Side Story*, which we were convinced might
bury us. The story was loosely based on the life of Tommy
Steele, substituting bongos for a guitar. The lead (*not* the title
role) was Paul Scofield, of whom we were in awe. At least,
until rehearsals, when we realised what a sweetheart he was.
Already a major RSC star, who had resisted overtures from
Darryl F Zanuck to go to Hollywood, he was an impressive
coup for the producers. He had never done a musical before,
so the whole venture was promising, to say the least.

Also in the cast were Millicent Martin, Charles Gray and
Victor Spinetti, with whom I was to work in the nightclub
shows. Bongo Herbert, the singer, was played by Jimmy
Kenney, son of a music-hall star, Horace Kenney. He had
just had a *succès de scandale* in a film called *Cosh Boy* which
reflected the juvenile crime scene of the day. He was so
convincing in it, that a woman hit him with a handbag at
the premiere.

A wonderful Jewish actor, Meier Tznelniker, played the
agent and sang two superb songs, 'Nothing Is For Nothing'
and 'Nausea', which remind me of Brecht and Weill (and
what an act they were). The show savaged the current pop
scene and was, in some ways, ahead of its time.

Paul, to the surprise of Burt Rhodes, the musical director, had almost perfect pitch, but rather erratic timing. That is to say, he had an innate ability to get a bar and a half ahead of the band. When this happened, Burt would cut the orchestra with a swift gesture and the pianist would carry on, until the rest of the band had worked out where he was.

Funnily enough, Tommy Steele's wife to be, Annie, was in the show, and he came to see it. Susan Hampshire, making her first West End appearance, played a debutante (a now extinct species, daughters of the upper crust, who were presented each year at the palace). Tommy, having watched a production that mercilessly parodied his own career, merely commented: 'Debs don't talk like that.'

On the first night in Newcastle, Paul delivered one of the best ad libs I've ever heard. At one point in the show, he had to enter Millie Martin's flat. This was, indeed, a 'flat', a piece of scenery with a door in it, secured by stage weights. As he entered, he would kick the door shut behind him. On this particular night, he duly kicked the door and the whole thing, very slowly, began to fall over.

Paul pulled Millie downstage and the scenery fell behind them, in a cloud of dust. The audience was still. Looking back, Paul said, 'Mice.'

Jimmy Kenney had a surging, religious ballad at the end of the first act, a hymn of praise to his mother entitled 'The Shrine on the Second Floor'. It was a wonderful piss-take of similar songs around at the time. On the first night in

Nottingham, we were ranged behind him, clad in cassocks and surplices, bathed in the light from a stained-glass window. There was not a titter from the audience during the first song, but rapt attention. At the end, there was thunderous applause. A postmortem was held. Paul suggested he should walk on immediately on the last note and say, 'That was lovely, wasn't it?' before they had a chance to applaud. Ever afterward, he did, and it got a big laugh. What this proves, I've no idea, unless it just proves the old show-business maxim: 'Tell them what you're going to do, do it and then tell them you've done it.' Ah well.

It was during *Bongo* that I made my first record. I had been taken on by Frankie Vaughan's manager, Paul Cave, and he secured me an audition with Fontana Records. I was accompanied by Frankie (in person, not on the piano), who was signed to the parent company, Phillips. Looking back, I'm sure that was the sole reason I got the contract, to 'keep Frank happy'. Frank himself would be the last to want this sort of forelock tugging, but sycophants are born, not made. So it came about that, one night after *Expresso Bongo*, I went to a basement near Marble Arch to commit to shellac (this was post-cylinder) my major opus, 'The Purple People Eater'.

This had been written by Sheb Woolley, an actor and country singer, who appears in *High Noon* as one of Frank Miller's gang, who were going to kill Gary Cooper. (Just filling in the background. All right, I'll get on with it.) This deathless aria was the *ET* of its day, about a creature from outer space who came to earth and – er – that's it. The voice of the extraterrestrial was supplied by Mike Sammes on speeded-up tape and I have to say, whatever you might be thinking, the record was absolutely terrible.

I met, for the first time in a recording studio, hardarsed musicians who had heard and seen it all. They must have looked at me and thought, 'Here's another one.' I also met people such as flautist and reed man Johnny Scott, trumpeter Stan Rodrick, drummer Jack Peach, and a guitarist and friend from the *Bongo* band, Judd Proctor. Stan was a man who, when told at a TV recording session that Cilla Black was ill and couldn't sing, replied, 'The first is news.'

Formidable company indeed. I made a point of ingratiating myself with them, confessing my ignorance of and newness to it all, and, like every musician I have ever worked with since, as long as you don't give them any shit they are invariably cooperative and friendly. I still remember a well-known star, saying to an equally well-known musical director, 'Was that the same key you played it in this morning?'

The MD's face never moved. 'I can assure you it was, Des,' he replied gravely.

We did several takes of the space epic and the recording manager, Jack Baverstock, entered the studio from his box. 'Flat as a bloody pancake,' he intoned. I was a star.

The record was released – or, rather, escaped – and was greeted with a wall of indifference, due to the fact that Sheb Woolley's original had quite rightly cornered the market.

Subsequently, I imagine because his version wasn't issued in Scandinavia for contractual reasons, my humble cover was released over there and for three weeks I was number one in Finland. I repeat, for three weeks, I was number one in Finland. All right, so they gave away a car with each record. After that, there was no starting me. My two follow-ups sank before they were made. The option was not taken up and another career was stillborn.

Years later I listened to an album made by Judy Garland at Carnegie Hall. I heard her sing a snatch, if you'll pardon the expression, of 'The Purple People

Eater' as a joke. Did I tell you I met Judy Garland? Yes, I did – or, rather, I implied it.

SIX

A LITTLE NIGHT MUSIC

IT MUST HAVE been around 1960 when I first met Danny. I'd been writing revues for the Fortune Theatre. I must point out that this was immediately prior to *Beyond the Fringe* at the theatre, which changed the face of revue as we knew it. The impact of Messrs Cook, Moore, Bennett and Miller was irreversible and we humble hacks had to look elsewhere. I was lucky.

Prior to writing for the Fortune Theatre, I had spent some time 'between jobs'. I wasn't just resting; I was virtually in a coma. I bummed around, picking up whatever odd bits of work I could – and some of it was very odd – and living in a variety of bedsits. I was sitting in one such gentleman's pied-à-terre one evening, contemplating whether to dine at the Savoy or the Ritz, when there was a knock at the door. It was my upstairs neighbour, Doug Camfield, who later went on to become a highly regarded TV director. Since we're both doing nothing, he suggested, why don't we write something together. So we sat down and started to write material for a television series for Scots comedian Jimmy Logan.

On reflection, I think I peaked early as a comedy writer. Doug and I submitted four unsolicited sketches to the show's producer and every one of them was accepted. A one hundred per cent hit rate. It was the first and last time that happened. Any comedy writer will tell you that, to survive in this game, you have to quickly become inured to rejection, which is often delivered in the most brutal and public manner.

When the Logan series ended, I returned to writing theatrical revues, helped along by the introductions made for me by an actress friend, Anna Quayle. One such revue – written with Ted Dicks – was *And Another Thing*, which was staged at the Fortune Theatre and starred Bernard Cribbins, Anton Rodgers and the formidable Joyce and Lionel Blair. Danny La Rue was in the audience one night and asked to meet Ted and me after the show. He invited us to write a show for him at the nightclub where he was starring – Winston's in Clifford Street off Bond Street in the heart of London's West End – and that's the longest address since Abraham Lincoln's.

We duly went to see the current show. As I remember, it featured a sketch concerning Lady Chatterley and the gamekeeper, Mellors, in which the immortal line 'I'm a pheasant plucker' occurred. One night, the girl who had to say it, who had been advised not to get a fixation about it, did, and the resultant spoonerism collapsed the audience. Ted and I had never been in a nightclub, never mind worked in one, and we were fascinated.

Firstly, the show didn't start until 1.15 a.m. and the place began to fill up from midnight onwards. Many of the clientele were, shall I say, interesting in appearance. Their faces bore the signs of spirited discussions with colleagues, during which hardware had been used. Get the picture? The rest of the audience was a mixture of show biz faces, businessmen and mysteries. 'Mysteries' were men and women of whom one knew nothing and who, by that very fact, were intriguing. They came to watch and listen. Some were writers; some weren't. One non-mystery was Wolf Mankowitz, a friend from the days when I appeared in *Expresso Bongo*. He wrote the book of that show and, as a keen student of the human condition, was a regular visitor to Winston's.

The show that night was bright, bawdy and exhilarating. Danny, whom I'd never seen in action, was a revelation. He made endless entrances (and *that* sounds like one of his lines) for a start. Every time he appeared on the tiny stage, he was attired in the most elaborate, exotic 'frocks', as he was wont to call them. The speed and skill of his changes astonished me. The stunning visual effect was accompanied by a deep baritone voice and a careful creation of the impression that he was more than friendly with the girls in the show.

This androgynous extravaganza fascinated me – this very masculine drag act – and we were to work on it for quite a few years to come. From 1961 to 1974, in fact, during which time Danny acquired his own club, rather neatly called Danny La Rue's, in Hanover Square.

But back to that first night. Ted and I had a drink with him in the noisy gloom of the club and we were hired. Arising the next day, with heads full of small men with hammers, we started to write. The mood, as I said, was bawdy and we had to adapt. I made the ritual phone call to my mother, to inform her that I was now a writer for a nightclub. Apparently, she told everybody about it, the profession of writer being obviously more acceptable than that of low comedian, my previous incarnation. The fact that most of the jokes I was writing were concerned with genitalia, and various basic bodily functions associated therewith, didn't seem relevant at the time. I was a writer. That was enough.

During rehearsals, the lead singer caught Ted's eye and, shortly afterwards, mine. She was called Terry Donovan and had appeared with Danny in pantomime, playing Prince Charming in *Cinderella*. Her legs were eloquent testimony of that, if indeed legs can be so described. Romance was soon to blossom, as you will shortly discover.

The show opened to a packed house. Danny was in control from the first moment, in spite of having neglected to commit most of his lines to memory. This was his usual practice, as he devoted all his time in rehearsal to his wigs and frocks rather than the script. He was steered through the show by splendid professionals like Toni Palmer, a veteran from Joan Littlewood days at the Theatre Royal, Stratford East. Ted, unfortunately, got involved in a fiscal altercation with the manager, an incredible Damon Runyonesque character called Bruce Brace and left after the first show, but I stayed on. We were soon joined by Ronnie Corbett.

SEVEN

THE ONE RONNIE

THE SCENE: DANNY LA RUE's club, situated in the top left-hand corner of Hanover Square, London, or, to put it another way, behind what was formerly Woolworth's on Oxford Street. I was writer in residence and also appearing in the show. Our curtain – there was nonesuch, just a small marble floor – went up at 1.15 a.m.

The jokes were, not to put too fine a point on it, *risqué*. In my defence, I must point out that I endeavoured to cloak my Rabelaisian epigrams in innocuous wording. For example, Danny La Rue in the persona of Lady Cynthia Grope – a Tory virago and predecessor of Margaret Thatcher, was asked what she thought of Michael Foot. 'A wild exaggeration!' Lady C replied. All right, you had to be there. 'Let's talk about Edward Heath . . . and people do, you know,' the speaker continued. You get the idea?

Please remember, this was the sixties. The hoary cliché opines that if you can remember the sixties you weren't there. Well, I can and I was. Danny's club was frequented by many of the cult figures of the day: Noël Coward, Judy Garland,

Princess Margaret and the then Tony Armstrong Jones, and, on one memorable night, Margot Fonteyn and Rudolph Nureyev.

Dame Margot came to see one of our shows, which included a subtly understated piece written by yours truly, in which Dan and Ronnie portrayed Fonteyn and Nureyev. Dame Margot was presented as an aging nympho and Nureyev as a petulant queen. You can tell I tended to prefer the broadsword to the rapier. Dame Margot, to my immense relief, was amused and mooted the idea that she would like to book the club for a private party. This had never been done before, but Dan readily agreed. The guests were to be herself, Nureyev and the Australian Ballet Company, with whom they were then appearing in London.

Dame Margot insisted that the relevant number be retained. I was now acutely apprehensive. She had enjoyed it, but would Nureyev? Would the company? Or would they, like the audiences at the old Royal Command shows, look to see if the monarchy were laughing before they dared to?

In the nightclub show at that time was the actor Doug Fisher, whom Dan had spotted in a Cambridge revue. Doug had a degree in Russian and spoke it fluently. I suggested that he should introduce the ballet item in Russian for the benefit of Nureyev, whose English at that time was somewhat sparse.

Came the night and the place was heaving. So was I. The club was packed with the company, friends, lovers, Dame

Margot's husband, Roberto Arias in a wheelchair (he had been paralysed in an attack by political opponents), Dame Margot herself and the legendary Nureyev. I lurked in the darkened doorway that was our only entrance on to the floor, listening for audience reaction. The show was going well, but the outrageous, not to say libellous, *pas de deux* was yet to come. The moment arrived.

Doug went on and began his Russian introduction. The main part of the audience was obviously baffled, but Nureyev was loving it. I later found out that Doug's speech was filthy. I was cock a hoop (what *does* that mean?). Doug left the floor and Ronnie entered, bewigged and wearing tights that could only be described as outstanding.

Digression. Two small children were watching Nureyev on television and the little boy, pointing at Rudolph's most prominent feature, asked his sister, 'What's that?' 'That's for the lady to stand on, when she wants to go up,' she told him.

Back to the club. Danny entered as Dame Margot. His characterisation bore not the slightest resemblance to the original, apart from the tutu and wig, but the effect was hilarious. Dan and Ron's performances were greeted with gales of mirth and I relaxed. Then I noticed that something strange was occurring. Rudolph was sitting next to a friend, who was translating for him, which led to a fascinating exercise in delayed reaction. When a joke got a laugh from the rest of the audience, Rudolph's face remained impassive until it was explained to him. Then he would roar with laughter some fifteen seconds after everyone else. This, in turn, would cause the audience to laugh at him laughing. We'd never had so many laughs – we were getting three per joke! Oh, blissful night.

I will always cherish the memory of Margot Fonteyn revelling in this scandalous portrayal, instead of rushing to her lawyers. The night was euphoric.

I worked with Nureyev some time later, at Elstree, when he performed with a new partner, Ulli Wuhrer of the Vienna State Company. She was taller than him, which he found unpleasing. During rehearsal, she missed her mark twice and he hit her. She fled in tears and he came up to the director's box, put his feet on the desk and, with great *élan*, asked for raw steak. Raw steak in Borehamwood on a Sunday afternoon? Some was found – of course it was. These people aren't like the rest of us, you know.

Footnote: As before noted, Danny's club was behind what used to be Woolworth's in Oxford Street. One night, Ronnie Corbett's mother and father came to see the show. Good Scots folk, proud to see their son in full cry. Danny, as ever, was the perfect host and they were given a front table, champagne, the works. After the show, Danny, Ronnie and I went to sit with them. Ronnie's father was glowing. Looking around the small room and remembering its location, he said to Danny, who was by then ruling the West End's club world and already a big star: 'You're wasting your time here, son.'

EIGHT

NAME DROPS AND ROSES

As PREVIOUSLY MENTIONED, the stage at Danny's club was a small marble circle, and the band were squeezed into an even smaller stand off to one side, curtained off from the main room so as not to offend the sensibilities of the customers.

Towards the end of her sad and turbulent life, Judy Garland was appearing at the Talk of the Town – now the Hippodrome – in London. Plagued by ill-health and only half aware of where she was some of the time, she was still a big draw. Some nights she didn't appear, so they had an act standing by to deputise for her.

'Who was that?' I hear you ask. Well, it was Lonnie Donegan. Yes, the obvious replacement. One night, I was told by the publicist, Glyn Jones, a woman in the audience shouted, 'You're drunk!' at the great star.

'Come on then, honey, you give us a song,' countered the indefatigable Judy.

The woman climbed on the stage and sang 'Somewhere Over the Rainbow' beautifully. I break out in a sweat even thinking about it.

The night Judy Garland came to Danny's club, he introduced her to the audience and invited her on to the minute cabaret floor to say a brief hello. She graciously took the microphone, had a quick word with the band and proceeded to regale us with at least three numbers while Dan surrendered and sat at a table. I think that is the memory of her I would like to preserve.

A *frisson* of panic ran through the cast the night Noël Coward walked in. Part of the show was a tribute to Coward and ended with a rousing Noël Coward finale. We had, however, taken the liberty of adapting some of his songs and writing new lyrics for others. I have to say that performing 'Don't Put Your Daughter on the Stage Mrs Worthington' while its creator sat not four feet away from me was one of the most nerve-racking moments of my career.

Throughout the show he sat puffing a Marlboro cigarette and watching with those hooded eyes set in a mandarin face. He was a wonderful audience, laughing and applauding at every opportunity. The finale arrived. Dan, Ronnie and I sang his numbers right in front of him, as did Annie (Ron's wife), Toni Palmer and the rest of that brilliant company. Not a venture for the faint-hearted. He beamed.

After the show, we were told that Coward wanted to see us. The backstage arrangement was that Danny had the star dressing room and everybody else shared the only other dressing room. It was here that we lined up, like naughty schoolboys, to await our fate. Coward walked in and we all said, 'Hello.'

'Now,' he said, 'who was responsible for that finale?'

Bravely, we all shouted, 'Bill!' and pointed at Bill Solly, the show's musical director (who now tells me he wasn't even there!)

'Very good, very good,' said Coward.

I thought Bill was going to die of pleasure.

'And did you do the one about the callgirls as well?' he asked.

'No,' said Bill, 'that was Barry.'

The smile faded from my face. In my panic I had forgotten that we had abused another Coward piece, for which I had written new lyrics about the activities of callgirls and Danny had dressed up as a hooker. He regarded me for a moment and then patted me on the head.

'Nearly as good as mine,' he said.

He stayed chatting to us for two and three quarter hours. I know; I timed it. He wasn't witty or waspish or world-weary or indeed anything else beginning with W. He was charming, avuncular, interesting and interested.

When Noël Coward was introduced to my wife, Terry, for the first time, she was very pregnant with our first son. Coward patted her on the stomach and said, 'Here's to a wonderful opening.'

Talking of Noël Coward, I once did a warm-up for a TV show which was a David Frost interview with Coward. Now there's a superfluous job – going on to talk to a studio audience before one of the world's greatest talkers comes on. I did my usual preamble and was then informed that a camera had broken down. Keep talking. I talked on and on. I gradually ground to a halt. The nerves of the evening took hold of me. I walked upstage, to where a bottle of champagne and a bucket of ice awaited the arrival of the great men.

'God, give me a line,' I prayed. I looked down into the bucket and then up again. 'Monogrammed ice cubes?' I said, in disbelief. It got a laugh, I swear. Then the camera was restored and the show started. I take no credit for the line, such as it was; sometimes an outside agency seems to take over and gives you the thought. I remember being heckled, persistently, by a drunk one night and in sheer desperation I heard myself saying, 'Oh, piss off.' I suppose it's a gift, really.

Another surprise guest at Danny's one evening was John Lennon, who walked in, not with the other Beatles, but in the almost equally illustrious company of Peter Sellers, Lionel Bart and Marty Feldman. Lennon was completely out of it and as soon as I saw him I thought, We're in for a lively night here.

I was not wrong. Lennon heckled every act that came on, including the female singers and dancers, who are not, traditionally, best placed to respond to that sort of behaviour. Not to put too fine a point on it, I was not impressed.

Some years later I was working on the Frost show when Lennon was a guest. By now he was well into his peace and love phase and was evidently a far more mellow man.

He approached me before the show began, studying me intently. 'I know you, don't I?' he said. 'But where do I know you from?'

I reminded him of that night in Danny's club.

'Oh, God, I didn't, did I?' he groaned. 'To be honest with you, I don't remember a lot about those days.'

We sat down and I had a very pleasant chat with this charming, witty and thoughtful man. Not for the first time, I was forced to alter my opinions radically.

John Osborne was one of the many celebrity regulars at Danny La Rue's, and when he invited me to one of his famous parties I eagerly accepted. I invited my eldest son to join me, partly because he had just passed his test and could drive me down to John's home in Robertsbridge, East Sussex.

The party, which was held in the grounds of the house, was a glittering affair, packed with literary and theatrical heavyweights including Ralph Richardson and Michael Horden. My son was so impressed.

These were the exalted circles in which his father moved? The impression was reinforced when John emerged from the house, arms held open in greeting. 'Barry, Barry,' he growled, cupped my face in both hands and French-kissed me. There are no words a father can offer to his son at a moment like that.

NINE

FAMILIAR FACES

THE UNDERLYING THREAD of this erratic narrative is my family. As I mentioned earlier. I met Terry Donovan at Winston's nightclub, off Bond Street, in 1960, at rehearsals for the first show I wrote for Danny La Rue, who introduced us. My musical partner, Ted Dicks, had already pointed her out to me as she stood by the piano. I was immediately smitten. At the time, I was having one of my periodic bouts of severe eczema. (Mills and Boon, this book isn't.) I was wearing dark glasses and, due to a stiff neck, was unable to turn my head without moving my whole body. An alluring picture. To further heighten the impression I must have created, I had written a lyric for Terry on the subject of certain substances, entitled 'That Old White Magic'. She must have thought she was meeting William Burroughs.

Soon we started 'going out' together – I love the paradox of that expression, when the greatest joy of a relationship is 'staying in' – and one day we were dogsitting. We were in Hyde Park, walking five of our charges. It was raining, Terry had been for a job, unsuccessfully, and I thought, I'll cheer her up! I'll propose! Male ego or what?

She said, 'I can't answer a question like that now – I'll tell you tomorrow.'

The next day dawned. We were in the park again.

'The answer to your question is yes,' she said.

Dear reader, if you have had an alarming premonition, you're right. I replied, 'What question?'

She hit me with a dog.

We're still together, 47 years later. Tony was born in 1963 at St Mary's Hospital, Paddington, while I was appearing in the nightclub show. Dave followed in 1965, daughter Jacqui in 1968 and Bob in 1973. Granddaughter Ruby made her appearance in 1991, and in 1999 grandson Evan arrived, followed later by Tom, Archie, Hope, Martha and Constance. The current score is four children and seven grandchildren after extra time.

Their father (BA English Literature failed, as you recall) is proud of the degrees notched up by the gang. I think they learnt by my example and decided to complete my unfinished business. Ruby wants to be a balancer.

We live in the hub of the universe, Hatch End in Middlesex. Our house was built in 1900 and we owe it to Ronnie Barker, who used to live nearby and suggested a tour of the 'For Sales'. The owner was an orchestral flautist and I beat him down from £11,000 to £10,400. This was in 1967,

I must add. The past is a different country, and they do things differently there.

I never tried to encourage or discourage any of our children about going into the magic world of show business; I just wanted them to be happy at whatever they did. They have made me happy, which as a less-than-perfect husband and father is more than I deserve.

Garry Morecambe, son of Eric, once wrote that he remembered his father as a man going out of the door, putting his coat on. That rings a knell with me. Terry has run the home and family and for that I shall be ever grateful. In fairness to myself, I have to say I have made all the big decisions through the years, whether China should be admitted to the United Nations and so on. I love the business I'm in, or, rather, the people. My old friend, David Nobbs, when rather emotional one night, said, 'God, I hate show business.'

His wife said, 'You love it, that's what you hate.'

TEN

A PACKET OF PLAYERS

WHEN I WAS newly married I had an audition at the Players'
Theatre in Villiers Street, London WC2. This was, and is,
a theatre specialising in music hall in the Victorian/Edwardian
tradition, or, rather, an idealised picture of the same. As I
said, I was newly married and my wife, Terry, had also auditioned for the Players'. She got the job; I didn't. I sang 'I'm
Henry VIII I Am' and, obviously realising I was an impostor,
they turned me down. However, a week or two later, I got a
call to say that they were without a chairman for the following
week. The chairman is the MC of the proceedings, resplen-
dent in tailcoat, frilly shirt and white gloves, banging his
gavel to announce the acts. This elegant creation was virtually invented at the Players' Theatre; the original chairmen
were pub landlords, hardly the epitome of sophistication. The
master practitioner was Leonard Sachs, who invented the
tradition whereby the chairman used a string of long words
to bedazzle the audience and fill in time. He went on to
appear in *The Good Old Days* on BBC television, a broad
commercial version of the theatre show.

So, after failing my audition, I was offered a job. I went along on the Monday afternoon and was taken through the ritual: when to light and blow out candles, how to respond when a train roared by overhead (the theatre was under the arches of Charing Cross Station), how to respond to hecklers ('Oh, piss off' was not recommended. In fact, James Robertson Justice, one of the early chairmen, used to reply in classical Greek) and other arcane activities.

I got through my first night on automatic pilot. It's amazing how nerves can anaesthetise you and give a completely false impression of confidence. I was coached by one of the resident chairmen, Maurice Browning, who had contracted polio in the desert during the Second World War and thus walked with a pronounced limp. (Pronounced 'limp'.) Maurice, who was bald, wore an amazing blond wig which was rumoured to have a life of its own. He was a good friend with an acid wit. One night, a customer lurched up to him and said, 'Can I tell you a joke, Maurice?'

'I doubt it,' said Maurice.

The Players' Theatre was a good school and I learnt about the handling of audiences, celebrating birthdays, anniversaries, divorces, greeting visitors, etc. This supplemented what I had learnt at the Windmill, i.e. not to be afraid of silence. After some three years of working there, I was approached at the bar by one of the older members after the show. 'Quite good,' he said.

'Thank you,' I improvised.

'You must be one of the new ones,' he said.

Ah, well.

Clive Dunn, later to achieve fame in *Dad's Army*, was an alumnus of the Players' and still made occasional appearances. Some lines from his act I remember still. His opening was: 'It's not only a great pleasure to be here, it's rather inconvenient' and 'I met an old man working in the gents at the Café Royal who had met Oscar Wilde. I asked him what the great man was like. "Very nice," he replied, "but a bit of a pig with the free Brilliantine."' (For younger readers: Brilliantine was a predecessor of Brylcreem, available from a dispenser in the gents. Much favoured by Irish playwrights of genius.)

Not the most generous of employers, the Players' was nevertheless regarded as the best labour exchange in London (labour exchange means job centre) where you could spend your wages in the bar and get your National Insurance card stamped. I'll never forget the friends I made there and the sheer camaraderie of the performers.

During this period I was still working at Danny's club. After a gruelling evening introducing acts, greeting overseas visitors ('Australia, sir? How does it feel to be [here the audience joined in] the right way up!' The spirit of Wilde lived on), celebrating birthdays, anniversaries, divorces, etc., I would wash off my make-up, remove the side whiskers, have a drink and then walk through the West End after midnight, to the club in Hanover Square. There I would promptly reapply my make-up. I can't remember when I last wore make-up on stage, but I still have a crumbling stick of greasepaint at home that I intend to auction at Sotheby's.

The show at Danny's would start, of course, at around 1.15 a.m. After a while, this routine was beginning to take its toll, so I reluctantly left the Players' Theatre. I still appear there from time to time; on the last occasion with Peter Ustinov, to celebrate the theatre's sixtieth anniversary.

I was on the *Good Old Days* TV programme several times, either solo or in a double act with Bernard Cribbins, and it was a pleasure to be back at the City Varieties in Leeds, where I had had my first job all those years before. It's the oldest music hall in Britain and boasts the statutory ghost.

On several occasions, I was in one of the dressing rooms on the upper floor and established a record for getting to the circle bar in thirty seconds. This involved dashing through a small door, along a catwalk above the stage and up the side of the circle into the bar. However, my early attempts at the record were hampered by an inexplicable slowing down as I ran along the catwalk and a distinct chill in the atmosphere. I was informed this was the resident ghost.

I once spotted a figure in the circle during rehearsals at the Tyne Theatre in Newcastle, which had been a music hall, and was assured there was nobody there at the time. The crew were convinced that I had seen Harry, a carpenter at the theatre in the early part of the century. In those days, sound effects were fairly primitive and, if the sound of thunder was required, a cannon-ball was thrown into a revolving drum. One night, it was lobbed too vigorously, bounced off and struck Harry on the head, killing him. They told us he often popped in to watch rehearsals and was inclined to tidy up if anyone left a mess. The Theatre Royal, Bath, has its butterfly. The play *Jeffrey Bernard is Unwell* by Keith Waterhouse played its first week there and apparently the butterfly landed on Peter O'Toole's head during a rehearsal. This was a good omen, but if a dead butterfly is discovered the reverse is true.

When Willie Rushton and I played at the theatre, we had heard of the legend. Willie acquired a butterfly in a glass case. As I told the audience the saga, Willie walked on behind me displaying the case to the audience, shouting, 'Got the bugger!'

After the show, one of the stage crew took me to one side. 'Never mock the butterfly,' he said.

I reminded him that it was Willie and not I who had done the deed. The next time I played there, I was told that my mother had rung the stage door asking for me. She had died several years before. When my wife and I arrived at Leslie and Jean Crowthers', where we were staying the night, there on the window sill of our room was a dead butterfly. Excuse me, there's someone at the door. I think.

I was happy and settled at Danny's. I had a new wife and a growing family and was contentedly employed in the noble and honourable task of writing gags about men's genitalia.

That is what I did: I was a cock-joke writer. I was not ashamed of it and I was happy doing it.

One night at Danny's, we were informed that David Frost was in the audience. Already, due to *That Was the Week That Was*, a TV eminence, his presence caused a mild stir. Frost jokes were circulating even then. He was alleged to have an open-top, convertible car with a button on the dashboard. If it started raining, he pressed the button. And it stopped raining . . . This was a portent of the power he was to wield as he became a member of the establishment he had spent so much time mocking. I've noticed this phenomenon elsewhere. Jonathan Miller and John Cleese both now bear a startling resemblance to the sort of people they used to pillory.

Back to the plot. After the show . . . (That could have been the title of this book. My memories of post-performance encounters are often much clearer than those of the shows themselves. Doctors call this see-you-in-the-bar syndrome and I have suffered from it, very happily, for many years.) After the show, he reiterated, I met David Frost for a drink and he invited me to write for a TV special he was about to do, wittily yclept *A Degree of Frost* – no relation to the David Jason vehicle laying waste to the ratings at the time of writing. After the special, I was enlisted for the writing team on *The Frost Report*, a new weekly series.

I soon met my fellow scribes: David Nobbs, a journalist, later to become a writing partner when we worked on Les Dawson shows and, of course, the author of *Reggie Perrin*;

the late Dick Vosburgh, one of the funniest men I knew, an expat American whom we managed to import – or whatever the opposite of 'deport' is; and the whole of what was to become *Monty Python's Flying Circus* – John Cleese, who was also in the show, Michael Palin, Terry Jones, Eric Idle and Graham Chapman.

Graham was also to become a partner and friend when we wrote some fifty sitcoms together for Ronnie Corbett, long before *Sorry*. These rejoiced under the title *No, That's Me Over Here*. Cryptic or what? The reason for this was that the original opening credits featured a school photograph and, as the camera panned over it, Ronnie's voice was heard saying, 'No, that's me over here.' This made perfect sense until, for a subsequent series, they dispensed with the school photograph and Ronnie's voice-over, retaining only the title. You can imagine the confusion this caused, resulting in one of the most misquoted titles in sitcom history. Therefore, I still gladly take credit for writing, 'No, Here I Am', 'No, This Is Me Over Here', 'That's Me There' and various other permutations.

The association with Graham was a long and happy one. Working on the *Doctor in the House* series among others, we practically became stitched at the hip. This rugby-playing, pipe-smoking son of a policeman from Leicester came out during our writing days together and threw a party to introduce us to his partner, David. At first, endearingly militant, he put money into *Gay News* and would invariably introduce himself: 'Good evening, I'm a homosexual.' He mellowed considerably and later informed me he was one hundred per cent bisexual, if you see what I mean.

He was an alcoholic, but even in his wildest excesses ever charming, albeit prone to dropping his trousers at inappropriate moments.

David Frost threw one of his excellent parties at one of the London hotels where guests descended a staircase into a room, having had their names declaimed in stentorian tones by an imposing toastmaster. Graham, and, to be fair, myself had indulged in some enthusiastic pre-party preparation and were in rosy mood. As we approached the red-coated master of ceremonies, he leant in for our names.

Graham whispered to him.

'Enoch Powell and Mrs Harry Belafonte,' the toast-master duly boomed.

We descended the stairs to a mixed reception. Graham, I miss you.

He died some years later, not having had a drink for a long time, but still joyfully visiting pubs with me. Looking back, to the boy dancers at the Windmill, the Players' Theatre, the gay ambience of Danny's club and working with Graham and Kenny Everett, I realise that some of my happiest memories are of working with and knowing my homosexual friends. The pleasure of their company embraces the word 'gay' in all its connotations.

I remember Ev saying to me once, 'Married thirty years and four children? What a smokescreen!' He also described me as 'honorary gay', which, coupled with a friend dubbing me 'honorary Jewish', gave me two of the most enjoyable compliments of my life.

From *A Degree of Frost*, I went to work on *The Frost Report* and *Frost on Sunday*. Those not old enough to remember will have gathered that there was a lot of Frost about at the time and he was the biggest thing on British TV in the mid-sixties.

Ever ambitious, David formed his own production company, Paradine Productions, which took me under its wing, together with artists such as John Cleese and a couple of comedians who were always known around the office as the two Ronnies – Messrs Barker and Corbett. David sold the idea of a show featuring them both to the BBC, where they became the upper-case 'T', and I was drafted in to write on the show. I have a lot to be grateful to David for. If you were a 'Frost writer', it opened every door, whether you were good, bad or indifferent. Fortunately, I was all three.

It was through the Frost association, via John Cleese, that I met up with the disparate talents who were to coalesce into *Monty Python*. Of course, I formed a particularly close relationship with the late Graham Chapman, with whom I wrote three series of the aforementioned *No, That's Me Over Here* and many episodes of *Doctor in the House*, a series which was also graced with the writing talents of John Cleese, Graeme Garden and Bill Oddie.

Monty Python was the raucous offspring of two successful shows: *Do Not Adjust Your Set*, which featured Michael Palin, Eric Idle, Terry Jones, David Jason and Denis Coffey; and *At Last the 1948 Show*, which included John Cleese, Graeme Garden, Marty Feldman and Tim Brooke-Taylor. With the judicious and farsighted guidance of Barry Took, out of this fabulously talented group of individuals emerged the show that was to change the face of British comedy for ever, or till a week the following Wednesday.

NEVER MIND WHAT I THINK, THE LISTENERS LOVE HIM

By Humphrey Lyttelton

I HAD NEVER met Barry Cryer before *I'm Sorry, I Haven't a Clue*, though his reputation as one-time vocalist with the Leeds University jazz band had reached me, despite all my evasive efforts, many years earlier. Indeed, although we shared the chairmanship of *Clue* during its very first series, I knew him only by his voice until he joined as a regular panellist. And what a voice, capable, like the cornet of the legendary Buddy Bolden, of being heard fourteen miles away across Lake Ponchartrain on a clear night!

Never mind what I think; the listeners love him. On my travels around the country wearing my musician's hat, I'm always asked questions about the programme, some of them predictable: 'Heard from Mrs Trellis lately?', 'What are the rules of Mornington Crescent?' and (this one with a ghastly leer) 'How's Samantha?' I'm sick of explaining that, as far as I'm concerned, she seems to suffer from a perpetual headache. Perhaps the commonest question is 'Does Barry enjoy the show as much as he sounds?' I can't answer that, since it's my job as chairman to see that everyone enjoys it as little as possible. But, short of a seizure, I can think of no other explanation for that laugh. 'Cluck' is the word that springs to mind, but it's quite inadequate. Henlike, yes, but a hen that has had a brief, injudicious but fertile liaison with an ostrich and is now paying the excruciating price.

But, of course, he's lovely, and I'm grateful to him for many things, not least the occasions all too frequent when my mind goes totally blank for seconds on end (they call it 'timing' but I know better) and he brings me and my career back from the brink of disaster with a cry of 'Nurse, the screens!'

ELEVEN

THE AURAL DANCE

I DID MY first radio show while working with David Nixon in the pantomime. I was selected, after an audition, to appear in a programme for BBC Radio Manchester. It was called *Search for a Star* and the compère was a well-known actor, Jack Watson. He had been formerly known as Jack 'Hubert' Watson, as he had worked in an act with his father, playing the part of the son, Hubert, on stage. His father, a star in his day, bore the stage name, Nosmo King. He got the idea when he saw two doors, with the words 'NO SMOKING' on them. When the doors were ajar, this became 'NOSMO KING'. Great story, eh!

Moving rapidly along, I journeyed to Manchester on the appointed Sunday and did my piece to a reasonable reaction from the audience. They were then, in time-honoured fashion, asked to vote. The winner was a tenor, Victor Labatti. However, subsequently, I won the listeners' vote and was invited to the final, to be held some weeks later. By then I was at the Windmill and couldn't take part. Where are you now, Victor? I salute you.

Radio didn't play a part in my life again until two years later, when I was appearing in *Expresso Bongo* (qv). I had, by then, passed my radio audition. Many years later, I was given a report made at the time. It said 'A pleasing personality'. At least I think it did – the parchment had faded somewhat.

The show I was booked for was rather accurately entitled *Midday Music Hall*, as it was, in fact, a music-hall programme, broadcast at, er, midday. The star was the amazing Max Miller and I arrived at the Playhouse Theatre in London to discover I was sharing a dressing room with him. I must point out that dressing rooms have never been the norm on radio shows. After all, what costumes and make-up do you need? But the great Miller insisted on wearing his stage costume – a flamboyant suit with a design reminiscent of loud wallpaper, a white hat and what we used to call 'co-respondent shoes'. These were two tone and apparently assumed to be worn by the guilty parties or co-respondents in divorce cases. Stick with me, chums, and you'll learn more than you ever wanted to know.

Anyway, I was in awe of Miller. He was a giant of the music hall and had also made several films, in which he appeared to be ad-libbing. A massive star in the South of England, he made occasional forays up North, including to Leeds. In those pre-television days, comedy was much more regional than it is now, and comedians from one part of the country would often find it hard to register in another. Not Miller. My mother, of all people, seemed to have a soft spot for this outrageous maverick, who was regarded as the ultimate alternative. She took me to see him at the Empire. How that name recurs in this saga. The Empire strikes back . . . and back . . . and back.

She obviously got a charge from his deadly grin, what one critic described as 'his dreadful liquid eye' and his endless stream of innuendoes. Miller's material would seem tame today – he invariably left the audience to fill in the subtext – but his sheer charisma and command were something to see.

Meanwhile, back at the Playhouse, I was sharing a room with a god. He was friendly and unassuming. He suggested a cup of tea. I floated on a pink cloud. We went aloft to the minute tea bar. In the course of the morning, which included a trip to the Sherlock Holmes pub in Northumberland Avenue, he took me for three cups of tea, half a pack of cigarettes and two beers. I was honoured.

Roy Hudd told me that, when he was half of a double act, they appeared with Max and he invited them to join him for a drink in the circle bar between the shows. On entering the bar, he made straight for a table and sat down. They joined him. No mention was made of buying a drink. Soon, the customers for the second show began to drift in. 'Maxie! What are you having?' they asked.

'I'll have a scotch and these two'll have a beer,' Max promptly replied. He turned to the young Hudd and said. 'Let them buy it, it gives them a thrill.'

Have I painted the picture? To balance the portrait, I was told he often visited Brighton magistrates' court incognito and paid the fines of drunks and vagrants. In fact, on the day we worked together, he informed me that he was not disposed to buy drinks for seventeen strangers, only for friends. Fair enough.

During the rehearsal for the radio show, Max told a joke about a bus breaking down. This was in the days when buses had a driver and conductor/tress. The driver lifted the bonnet to discover the cause of the breakdown. After ten minutes, the conductress, looking at the impatient passengers, joined him and asked, 'Do you want a screwdriver?'

'No, we're ten minutes late already,' replied the driver.

Innocent stuff indeed but, in 1958, not the stuff of which live radio shows were made. The producer held his head in his hands and nervously asked Max to delete the joke from his act. He was greeted with a cheery nod. We repaired to the Sherlock Holmes. Ray Ellington, who appeared in *The Goon Show* with his quartet, bet Max five pounds that he wouldn't tell the joke on the programme. Max, with some reluctance, drew a note from his wallet and the picture of the Queen blinked in the light. The wager was made. During the show, we gathered on the side of the stage to witness the denouement. Max told several jokes, none of which involved a bus driver, sang a song and walked off to rapturous applause. We entered the Sherlock Holmes for the second time. Ray approached Max and demanded payment. Max said, 'I was going to tell it, but they flashed a light at me.' He wouldn't pay up. The moral of this story escapes me.

Some years later, I appeared in a radio sitcom called *Sam and Janet*; the title was culled from the joke about 'Sam and Janet Evening' (say it aloud) but that need not detain us here. I was nervous, still relatively new to radio, and at the rehearsal I fluffed and stumbled over my lines. Behind me, one of the stars said, *sotto voce*, 'It's never the same when someone new joins the team, is it!' Ah, the warm camaraderie.

Happily talking of warm camaraderie, for several years in the seventies I co-wrote and appeared in *Hello Cheeky* on the radio. My cohorts were John Junkin and Tim Brooke-Taylor, with Denis King in charge of the music. It was a joy to do, but BBC TV showed no interest. In those days, transferring from radio to TV was not a common occurrence – Tony Hancock being a notable exception – but we thought we had something. The powers at BBC Television Centre obviously thought we should keep it. So we crept away to YTV and made a thirteen-part series. We were on at eight o'clock on Monday night and I believe we put *Panorama*'s figures up. Ahead of our time ... or behind ... or who knows? But so enjoyable.

In 1972, I was approached by BBC Radio regarding a series called *I'm Sorry, I Haven't a Clue*, a spin-off from *I'm Sorry, I'll Read that Again*, featuring my friends from *Monty Python*, John Cleese and Graham Chapman, plus Graeme Garden, Tim Brooke-Taylor (again), Jo Kendall, Bill Oddie and

David Hatch, later to become a BBC supremo. They had all gone on to fame and fortune on TV, but radio wanted a follow-up. Graeme Garden suggested a silly panel game, requiring no scripts and very little rehearsal. Thus *Clue* was born.

In the first series, Humphrey Lyttelton, an inspired choice, and myself shared the duties of chairman, appearing in three shows each. The teams were taken from an amalgam of John Cleese, Jo Kendall, Bill Oddie, Tim Brooke-Taylor, Graeme Garden and myself, but subsequently the first three left, preferring to work with scripts, and a debate ensued as to replacements. I was pro- or, possibly, de-moted to panellist and, after very little discussion, Willie Rushton was invited to join. Twenty-four years later, in 1996, we were still together, with Colin Sell at the piano. Willie died in December 1996. John O'Hara, the novelist, said, when George Gershwin died, 'I don't have to believe it if I don't want to.' My sentiments exactly. More, much more of Will later.

Clue, described as the antidote to panel games, survives, or does as I write, because of . . . what? We enjoy it so much, I sometimes worry that we might sound indulgent, but listeners seem happy to join us. We've had our share of awards – we're just waiting for Lifetime Achievement. But our real reward is the knowledge that, maybe somewhere, we're helping someone forget their cares for a moment and realise that life can be . . . [breaks down, reaches for sick bag].

Humphrey Lyttelton used to come to Leeds in the fifties, and during my brief sojourn at Leeds University I went several times to hear the band at the town hall or the University Union. Little did I know, dear reader, he was to become an old and valued friend.

Like myself, Humph was in his anecdotage and told us that he had been relating for years the story of how he had played outside Buckingham Palace on VE Day. He admitted that he told that story so often he had no idea whether it was true or not. Two members of his band, devoted radio buffs, tracked down a recording, transcribed on to tape, upon which you can clearly hear him playing his trumpet behind commentator Howard Marshall. Humph said he was thrilled to have confirmation that it did really happen. In fact, he once heard a tape of me singing on the Leeds town hall steps with the university jazz band in 1955, so we can both sleep easier in our beds.

Humph, a birdwatcher, among his many other talents, was once interviewed on Radio Clyde in Scotland – where else? – during a period when he was a restaurant critic. The interviewer said, 'I believe, apart from your jazz and your writing about food, you're also a keen orthinologist.'

'Surely you mean word botcher?' replied Humph.

I guess you had to be there. He later admitted he thought of the line on the way out, but why let the truth get in the way of a good story? I never have – except in this book, of course, of which every word is true, I swear. I remember when I was asked to be a crew member for a Russian space probe . . . but that must wait for another time.

A few years ago Colin Sell, *Clue*'s music man, and I embarked on what is fallaciously described as a one-man show. This orgy of jokes, reminiscences and songs by me and Colin has taken us to many venues and settings. The very first time was at the Brewhouse, Taunton. You never forget the first time (see 'Windmill' earlier). It was half an hour before the show. Colin had gone off for his ritual walk to purchase fish and chips; Tristan Taylor, our promoter, was having drinks with the manager; and I was alone in the dressing room. Panic seized me. Was there going to be anyone out there? Could I entertain them for two hours? Even if I could, would they laugh? It was too late. The lights dimmed; Colin played and then introduced me. I walked on the stage . . . and that was the moment I woke up.

Woke up to the fact that it wasn't a dream. Two hours later, I found myself in the bar. Actually, it was easy – I was over in the corner. We've been doing the show ever since and I hope and believe that the audience enjoys it as much as we do.

Adam Wide, a friend and former stand-up, upon hearing I was doing a show, said, 'Are you doing the bucket?' This must rank as one of the more mysterious questions of our time. 'The bucket?' I queried. He then explained that the improvs ('the performers who extemporise around a theme or themes, suggested by the audience', *My Life in Comedy*, Paul Merton, 1982) have a bucket awaiting the audience as they come in. In this, they may place suggestions for subjects for that night's performance.

'How does that apply to me?' I asked.

'I've never mentioned anything but what it reminded you of something else,' he replied. (A portent of this book, dear reader, I'm sure you'll agree.)

So, to this day, our audiences are invited to place pieces of paper stating themes, subjects or sometimes just words, e.g. 'shirts' (it happened), in the bucket before the show. Upon these, I have to discourse during the second half. Whatever the outcome, the audience knows this is their part of the show – no faking – and, as a result, I have been known to wander into such flights of nostalgic whimsy that it has been suggested I have resorted to recreational chemicals. But that's enough about me, how are you?

TWELVE

WILLIE NILLY

As promised, I return to the subject of Willie Rushton. A very happy return. Like many old friends, Willie and I could never remember where and when we met. He always maintained it must have been somewhere round the back of David Frost. In the middle and late sixties, I was working with David on BBC and ITV and, of course, Will had been associated with him since *That Was the Week That Was*, so he could have been right about our first encounter.

But the first steady association started with *Clue* and continued until he left us in 1996. I'm still waiting for him to ring or walk in the door.

In 1991, Willie and I were discussing how the world was changing. Both of us, to say the least, had been around for some years, and we realised that TV was concentrating on younger performers. I was feeling the draught as a scriptwriter, because the current lot tended to write their own material. Will, a great pragmatist, said we should get off our arses and try to create our own work. The previous year, with Colin, Graeme Garden, juggler Pierre Hollins and singer Christine Pilgrim, we had put together an evening in aid of the Spinal Injuries Association, with which we toured the country. *Two Old Farts in the Night* was created from this, minus Graeme and Pierre, who had other commitments.

Will's son, Toby, was about to appear in a production of *The Duchess of Malfi* – or *What's It All About, Malfi* as Will called it – at the little Hill Street venue in Edinburgh, during the Fringe. Will rang the promoter and asked if he wanted a late show to follow *The Duchess*, and mentioned the two of us. The man readily agreed and *Two Old Farts in the Night* was, or were, born.

We travelled up to Edinburgh, somewhat apprehensive. This time it was for money – no goodwill, no warm 'charidee' glow. Will had drawn posters and we were ready to pound pavements handing out flyers (small posters) to passers-by. Some days, on the Fringe, there seem to be more people handing these out than anybody else. They finish up giving them to each other.

But, to our surprise and delight, we discovered that we were sold out for the week. Taylors Port, our sponsors from the SIA show, generously provided us with crates of the product, so the audience had a glass on the way in.

A thought about port. It's reputed to be a combination of aphrodisiac and tranquilliser. If you don't get it, don't worry about it. Oh, that evocative word 'it'; even in these PC days, writers still use it. That will be the first and last reference to political correctness in this book. As Victoria

Wood said, 'If it's bad taste, it isn't funny. If it's funny, it isn't bad taste.' I rest my case.

Anyway, we had a happy week. On the Thursday, we were told that a minion had rung to ask for ten seats for Neil Kinnock and party. They were told, with some satisfaction, that we were sold out. But they were found three. I had a Welsh joke in the show and, to this day, I'm convinced that the former Labour Party leader thought it was put in just for him. The Kinnocks stayed for some considerable time after the show and I watched Neil working the bar. To me, he told jokes. To two older men, he talked rugby. To Christine, our singer, he twinkled. A man for all reasons.

Back to Will. Was I ever away? His superb drawing skills and his wit on panel games were well known, but his mastery of stand-up comedy less so. He loved the theatre more than anything else and, during the seven years we did the show, I watched him blossom and grow, as I lost the will to live waiting in the dressing room for him to finish. No matter – he was funny. As Richard Ingrams said, he never changed but seemed to get better all the time. I sometimes thought I needed a set of jump leads to follow him, but I realised he *was* my jump lead.

The show was a haphazard *mélange* of jokes, songs and Will's spiralling imagination. We weren't a double act: when he walked off the stage, I walked on, and vice versa. But we met at the beginning and the end. I always remember we had a flaming row at the Theatre Royal, Plymouth, for whatever reason, and later I said to him, 'Now we're a real double act – we're rowing in the dressing room.' When we next played Plymouth, I said, 'It's our anniversary. This is where we had our row.'

'What's all this "we"?' he said.

Always the last word.

He would always go against a consensus of opinion, often just for mischief. I had a fantasy that somebody said to him, 'I hear you died in December, Will.'

'No, no, not me,' Will would have said.

Will and I used to follow each other round the after-dinner circuit and one evening a man asked, 'Willie Rushton's a friend of yours?'

I concurred, and he told me that Will had spoken at the dinner the previous year. He was sitting at the top table with their chairman, Sir Charles, who was giving Will's ear a vigorous bashing while he was eating his dinner. Will was murmuring 'Good lord' and 'I can imagine' and then the man said, 'You'd better be funny tonight, Mr Rushton. We're paying you a lot of money.'

'Well, most of it is for sitting with you,' replied Will.

We checked into the Europa Hotel in Belfast, a historic place which has been blown up at least three times. On the check-in form it said: 'How did you hear about this hotel?' Will wrote: '*News at Ten*.'

We arrived for one of our shows and, as was often the case, we met a piano tuner. He was blind. We chatted and after some minutes Will and I realised that we didn't like him. He was abrasive, pushy and, due to embarrassment and a certain amount of guilt, neither of us could think of a way to escape him – not even Will, who feared no situation. He clung to our side and even came with us to our dressing room. He was sitting with us, accompanied by his guide dog, as we got ready for the show. The atmosphere was tangible. Finally he got up and said, 'Well, I'll let you gentlemen get ready for your show,' and bid us good night.

As they left the room, Will said, 'How cruel of them to give you a cat.'

Will appeared in the production of *Treasure Island* at the Mermaid Theatre, playing the part of Squire Trelawney. Bernard Miles, who ran the theatre, was playing Long John Silver, and Eric Flynn the part of Dr Livesey. Will and Eric were on the stage and Will had a long speech about the evil sea cook, who had not yet made his appearance. Will lost his way – it was the first week of the run – and began, as he said himself, to ramble. He talked on and on and completely forgot to mention the crucial fact that Long John had only one leg. Finally, he ground to a halt. Eric Flynn looked at him.

'How many legs has he got?' said Eric.

Will, without a pause, replied, 'Well, you as a medical man would know that.'

His definitions of politicians were gems. To mention just two, he attributed Margaret Thatcher's behaviour to prime

ministerial tension and said he was convinced that John
Major believed that charisma was 25 December.

The very first night of *Two Old Farts in the Night* (charidee
version) was at the City Varieties Theatre, Leeds, scene of
my very first job, described in earlier pages. We were asked
to draw a raffle during the interval and Will drew the first
ticket.

'32 pink!' he cried, and up on stage came a good burgher
of Leeds – a small man, as I remember, in glasses. He took
the envelope containing a voucher from Will without a word.

'Have you a smile about your person?' queried Will, and
then, as the man made his way back to his seat, beamed at
the audience. 'Now for the next miserable Yorkshire bastard!'
boomed Will.

They loved it – but then, they always did.

We never knew about his heart. His diabetes was right up
front; we all knew about that, but not the state of his heart.
He was ordered to rest and I did two shows without him –
presumably one continuous fart in the night. I went to see
him in the hospital and he was delighted that I had told the
audiences that I felt like John Wayne Bobbitt – 'No Willie'.
(You'll recall JWB, whose wife unmanned him? Otherwise,
the line goes for nothing – *c'est la vie*, or 'say lavvy', as Kenny
Everett was wont to opine.)

He insisted on appearing in two recordings of *Clue* in
Cambridge and informed me that he was going to have his
'bloody plumbing' seen to the following week and would

ring me. The next day our former agent, Emma, rang and told me it was a triple bypass the next Tuesday. I was stunned. That day, I had my mobile switched on, frightened that it was going to ring. It did. He'd gone twenty minutes earlier. I had to go to the gents.

In the stage show, he used to say in the opening, 'People are always asking me what I want on my gravestone, particularly my wife, which is rather worrying. And then, the other day, I had a flash in Tesco's. I was wheeling my trolley round and there on a shelf was the very word I want on my gravestone. It said, "Discontinued".'

When I heard the news, I was in a pub with a pantomime cast. We raised our glasses in a toast: 'Discontinued.'

His ashes were buried under the boundary at the Oval and his memorial service was a riot. Endless laughs. David Kernan sang a hymn to fornication written by Will, and his son Toby read a piece Will had written about the birth of cricket. Humphrey's band played. The word 'celebration' was never more apt.

THIRTEEN

ONE MAN'S MATE IS ANOTHER MAN'S PYTHON

LOOKING BACK ON over fifty years of writing and performing – after all, what else can you do with it? – certain periods stand out as especially happy and eventful. Obviously, the night club days with Danny and so many good friends. Meeting Noël Coward, Burton and Taylor, Judy Garland, Fonteyn and Nureyev . . . I was going to call this book *Name Drops Keep Falling on My Head*, but Larry Adler got there first.

Working with Graham Chapman, whom I first met when we were part of the Frost writing roster at the BBC, was not to be forgotten. I think I wrote with him more than anyone else, outside the *Python* orbit. We penned over fifty sitcoms together, mostly for Ronnie Corbett, and episodes of *Doctor in the House*.

Basically a gentle man, he was, through most of the years we worked together, a formidable drinker, which tended to curtail the time available for writing. Come twelve o'clock, Graham would look at his watch and announce, 'Let's make it an early one,' and we would go up the road to the Angel in Highgate, with me realising the day had gone out of the window.

We once sat with Keith Moon of The Who in the Angel. I found him a very likeable man, admittedly on short acquaintance, with no sign of his famous excesses. He was good company. He suddenly said, 'Oh, I suppose they want a bit of Mooning,' not as in the current sense, trouser dropping, but as in 'Keith Mooning'. He stood up, gave a loud cry and smashed his glass on the floor.

A mild start from other customers, but the Angel was used to extrovert behaviour. The moment passed and the glass was cleared up.

As we left, Keith stopped at the bar and said, 'How much do I owe you for the glass?'

A pleasing symmetry.

I mentioned 'mooning' in its trouser-dropping sense and that was not unknown to Graham. At a party at Ronnie Corbett's, a rather tired and emotional choreographer performed a strip to the accompaniment of Denis King at the piano. As he approached his climax, if you see what I mean, his nerve failed him and he fled the room in a blur of pale flesh and gloomy Y-fronts. Graham rose. 'No finish?' he asked rhetorically, and dropped everything.

Danny covered the offending member with his handkerchief with a cry of 'For my next trick!', and Graham exited through the window into the rain. 'Never', 'dull' and 'moment' are the words that spring to mind.

We were in the bar at LWT and the sports department entered in festive mood. At the time, Jimmy Hill was leading them. Graham spotted them and announced that he wished to kiss the entire department. I loaded him on to a drinks trolley and wheeled him over. He went down the line, kissing each and every one. The men's faces were a picture – whether to respond or rebuff? Jimmy Hill was at the end of the line and as Graham approached he took the initiative and grabbed him in a clinch, bending him over backward. Applause ensued. I don't remember Graham actually offending anybody. Not in my company, anyway. The charm was constant.

In the bar at the BBC . . . (The locations may vary in this book, but the precise premises don't, as I'm sure you've noticed.) In the bar at the BBC, he reiterated, the wife of a well-known actor, who, for the sake of argument, I shall call James Villiers (the actor, not the wife), approached Graham and I and said hello. Jimmy was at the bar with a merry crowd, so she joined the writers for company. Graham looked at her breasts. 'Oh, beautiful,' he exclaimed, 'may I?' Before she could reply, or even work out what he meant, he cupped her breasts in his hands and beamed with pleasure. After a pause, so did she.

'That's the nicest thing that's happened today,' she said.

Around this time, Graham had come out, rather violently, and was already a formidable figure on the gay scene, but he always maintained that what it lacked was breasts, of which he was a devoted admirer. I could only envy his ecumenical fervour.

As the writing days contracted, and we were trying to complete scripts on the strength of about an hour's work a day, we drifted apart professionally, but, I'm happy to say, not personally. In the last ten or eleven years of his life, he didn't drink and coped stoically with his ever-present alcoholism.

Towards the end, I went to see him in hospital. I had adopted the ritual of taking him the most disgusting cake I could find, after discovering him looking aghast at some sticky confection left behind by previous visitors. We would consume these with great gusto and almost begin to enjoy them. One day as we finished off yet another culinary disaster, he looked at me and said, 'You know, Ba, I think death's overrated.' He certainly wasn't.

He died not long afterwards. When I told Willie that yet another writing partner had shuffled off the mortal coil, he said to me with a grin, 'You know what you are, Bazza,' he said, 'you're a bloody jinx.'

'Ba', 'Bazza', 'Bal' (in London) . . . I seem to be all things to all men and women, but I hope 'jinx' isn't one of them.

I can't start to remember any of my departed friends without laughing. Which brings me to Kenny Everett.

FOURTEEN

EVER EV

As with Willie, I can't remember exactly where and when I first met Ev, but I'm pretty sure it was at a lunch with Angela Bond, a radio producer, to discuss a programme that never happened (the vast majority). Ev and I hit it off straight [sic] away, but we didn't work together until much later. Ev had already had some TV adventures. His first series was *Nice Time* on Granada with Germaine Greer and Jonathan Routh from *Candid Camera*. The producer was one Jon Birt. Is the world ready for *two*? Later, he starred in *The Kenny Everett Experience* for LWT, but he still hadn't found himself in television terms.

I got a call to come and discuss writing a series for Thames, the premise of which was to use Ev as a video DJ, introducing guests, with jokes in between. The producer was to be David Mallett, whom I had worked with on Les Dawson shows, not to mention *Jokers Wild*. (But I will.)

During the preliminary chats, the name Ray Cameron was mentioned as an idea for someone to devise a game-show segment for the show. Ray and I had also worked together on *Jokers Wild*, which he co-devised.

We soon decided that he should be brought on board as a full collaborator as he and Ev had clicked instantly.

Does anyone remember 'Clicked' Well, they had, anyway.

The show was recorded without an audience, taping all day. No one shouted 'Quiet!' and any laughter from the crew was genuine. Also involved was the dance group Hot Gossip, choreographed by Flick Colby, and they were to prove a major attraction. The shows were enormously enjoyable to record and the joke element grew larger and larger. We soon realised we were making a genuine comedy show, not just DJ antics.

David Mallett's shooting of the Hot Gossip dance routines, up the crotch and down the cleavage, against stunning visuals, did suggest we would not be ignored. But we had no idea of the impact the show would have.

In its first year, with big star guests and Ev's manic links, which grew into full-blown sketches and characters, it was somewhat of a sensation. It won nearly every award going and the keen attention of Mary Whitehouse of the Viewers and Listeners Association. She condemned the show as pornography, which made the front pages and, of course, ensured increased viewing figures. We were on a roll.

I met Mary Whitehouse only once. We were introduced and I said, 'Thank you.' She seemed puzzled, so I explained. 'I work on the Kenny Everett Show and you made us. Thank you.' Her eyes double-glazed and she moved away.

Philip Jones, our boss at Thames, had, as I indicated, intended the show to be a vehicle for Ev as TV DJ and I don't think he quite appreciated the direction we were heading in. In fact, the joke at Thames at the time was that, if Philip ever found out the company were making the show, he would take it off. What a premonition. After a couple of series, just missing a Gold Rose at Montreux, and romps with the likes of David Bowie, Rod Stewart, Elton John, Bryan Ferry and many other luminaries of the day, we were on a high.

One of Ev's characters was an old rocker, Sid Snot, a name I had never liked, but I was outvoted. We conceived the idea of 'The Snots', a soap saga, consisting of a family clad exclusively in black leather who abused each other roundly and joyously (verbally, that is) and revelled in the tackiness. We almost got Diana Dors to play the mother, but she was filming a prehistoric epic, *When Diana Dors Roamed the Earth*, or similar.

We were due to record the first episode and arrived at the Teddington Studios. Our studio was empty. The sets were there, but no cast and no crew. We found out that Philip had been 'leaked' the script and had dismissed all concerned from work that day and cancelled the recording. Ev's face was a study in barely concealed rage. I knew the look; the face was calm but the eyes were cold steel.

We made our way to Philip's office, pausing only for tea and sticky buns and a chat with the trolley lady. Where are they now? Then back to business. We arrived at the office and Philip greeted us warmly and informed us that the offending item was no longer in the show. He then invited us to lunch, but Ev told him that we were lunching elsewhere and we left. Left Thames, as it turned out. At the end of the series, we went to the BBC.

I honestly think that Philip thought this was the biggest betrayal since Judas, but, when one remembers he poached Morecambe and Wise from the BBC, one is reminded, yet again, how nature balances itself.

It was not the same at the Beeb, it has to be said. Not in any way. We were embraced and they began the process of cloning Ev into a BBC comedian. Studio audience every Friday, pre-recorded sketches, nothing too naughty or messy, no rough edges, a finely honed product. Everything that Ev was not. Vast sets dwarfing modest jokes, lovely costumes and wigs, when asked for tat, the ultimate superb, professional back-up, which eventually destroyed everything we set out to do. It was over. The BBC lost interest and we certainly did. The small, pixy Ev persona hid a very complex, troubled soul. Once again, as with Graham Chapman, the pressures of coming out, coupled with the endless attention of the tabloids, began to take their toll. But the humour was irrepressible. We were visited once by a recording-company executive, whose name is mercifully erased from my memory. Ev took an instant dislike (the cold eyes). The man was sporting a large, ostentatious watch with five small windows at the base of the dial. These happened to be showing five zeros. Somebody asked him what they represented. 'That's his personality rating,' said Ev.

Another, similarly brash, man was part of a merry crowd in a restaurant, dominating and, at the same time, alienating the table. Ev, who had finished his food, announced he was leaving. Putting money on the table, he bid us good night. As he passed the brash one, he said, 'And good night to you.' With that, he lifted the man's plate of pasta and gently, as t'were Laurel and Hardy, pressed it into his face and left.

And there was, of course, the infamous Thatcher episode. There have been many accounts of this, and here's mine. We were filming *Bloodbath at the House of Death*, a film Ray and I had written for Ev, co-starring Pamela Stephenson and the living legend, Vincent Price (more of him later). It was a film that, had it not sunk to video within weeks, would have become part of horror-film lore. But enough of my unbiased opinion. Ev and I were sitting, as you do, in a wood outside Potters Bar and he informed me that Michael Winner had invited him to a Young Conservative rally at the Wembley Conference Centre the next Sunday. It was the run-up to the election and the blessed Margaret was to be present.

'Don't go,' I said.

'Why?' he, not unreasonably, asked.

'Because I know you and something will happen,' I replied.

This proved to be something of an understatement. Needless to say, he did go. He later told me that he was horrified by the audience: 'a Nuremberg rally' was his description and he came to the swift conclusion that they would cheer anything. Duly equipped with his enormous polystyrene hands (why did he take them? you may ask), he appeared on the platform.

'Let's bomb Russia!' he cried.

Hysteria.

'Let's kick Michael Foot's stick away!'

Mass frenzy.

Some misguided soul had asked him to introduce the leaderene. 'Now, it's time for megachick! I said to her this morning, "Margaret, that's no way to roll a joint!"'

Collapse of the Conference Centre.

Of course, it was on the TV news that very night and all over the papers the next morning. The *Daily Mirror*, I remember, had a two-headed Everett on the front page, one smiling, and one snarling: 'THE IDIOT FACE OF CONSERVATISM'.

David Steel, with a completely straight face, appeared on TV and, referring to Ev's Michael Foot remark, said it was disgusting to advocate attacking an old man. Ev was staggered by the reaction. His blend of shrewdness and naivety never ceased to amaze me.

'You'll never be allowed to forget this,' I said.

'Oh, it's tomorrow's fish and chips,' he said, not entirely convincingly.

But afterward, when interviewing him, journalists would invariably resurrect the incident and it became Ev's personal millstone.

I honestly don't think that Ev was a political animal. He told me he detested Margaret Thatcher, but, in general, he may well have leant more to the right. As opposed to your author, who was described by both the *Sunday Times* and the *London Evening Standard* as 'in the red corner' – but on what evidence? – Ev had an inborn sense of rebellion and would instinctively go against the mood of the mob. Like Graham Chapman and Willie Rushton.

Is there a theme emerging here about my favourite partners? You be the judge. A theme that is sadly emerging is the number of them that have gone.

Ev's sister rang one day and asked me to pop round to his flat in Earl's Court. I had been many times to find him cleaning or Hoovering and he was the ever-attentive host, rushing into the kitchen, putting the kettle on, looking for 'Mrs Ashtray' and generally settling me down. By now he had been diagnosed as HIV positive and had become increasingly ill. I entered the flat. This time he wasn't busying himself, but lying on the couch.

'Don't tell me how you are, you're a boring old queen!' I chortled, to hide my alarm.

Yet we talked and laughed as we always had done.

He suddenly said, 'Oh, Ba, we're scooping up all the gossip for the last time.'

I blew my nose. We embraced, and soon after I left. I never saw him again.

His funeral was a beautiful requiem mass and I was one of the readers. As I entered the church with his agent, Jo Gurnett, a helicopter flew overhead. We both said, almost in unison, 'He's late again.'

FIFTEEN

THE PRICE IS RIGHT

MY WIFE AND I became friends of Vincent Price and his agent, Arthur Marmor, and one night he was due to come to dinner at our house. Vincent was filming *The Abominable Doctor Phibes* at nearby Elstree and had accepted our invitation. He asked if he could bring Joseph Cotton along, who was in the film with him. At this news, Terry went weak at the knees. She had long harboured a passion for Joseph and attempted to comfort me by insisting that I reminded her of him. In a dark cellar at midnight, perhaps.

As if the possibility of her idol coming to dinner and her having to cook for the great gourmet, Price, wasn't enough, there was a power failure and all our electric appliances went down. Shortly after this, someone left the front door open and Jenny, our Irish setter, set off into the darkness in search of adventure. I did once say, 'Life is badly written.' No, thousands of times.

No cooking, no dog, utter blackness in every sense. We sallied forth into a Stygian Hatch End and eventually found Jenny. The lights came on and the oven was activated. Vincent and Arthur arrived, but no Joseph. But, please, you can't have everything. I mean, where would you put it?

The meal and the evening were a joy. Vincent was the perfect guest: 'I'm not leaving this house until I have that recipe,' he cried, and my wife did a passable imitation of a swoon. He then presented us with a book of worldwide recipes and went into the night.

Years later, he returned to appear in the Everett film and walked in on the first day to discover that my hair had changed colour in the interim. 'My God!' he said, 'the child has gone white in the service of comedy!'

One of my favourite memories is of an actor name-dropping relentlessly in the presence of Vincent during a break in filming. Vincent drew on his Marlboro. 'You appear to have mentioned everyone in the world, with the possible exception of two Popes,' he said.

When they made him, they drove a stake through the mould.

SIXTEEN

ON YOUR MARX

MENTION OF VINCENT Price's book, signed by the master, reminds me . . . (here we go again) of Groucho Marx. He was a long-time idol of mine and I had cherished the thought that one day we might meet, but considered it highly unlikely.

But wait! In the early seventies I was working at the Borehamwood studios of ATV, in what we writers described as the Des O'Connor incident. It was a six-month stint and the show was produced by a veteran American producer, Mort Lochman. Next door, they were recording *The Marty Feldman Comedy Machine*, an Anglo-American venture. ATV were very prone to these and I worked on several shows featuring American stars and near stars, who were sometimes unknown to the good burghers of Borehamwood and often struggled with the local audience. The comedian Dickie Henderson said that the shows were made for England and America and fell with a dull splash in the middle of the Atlantic.

Back to the plot. One week, Marty, whom I had known since the days of *The Frost Report*, informed me that

Groucho Marx was coming over the following week to appear on the show. My heart pounded, my pulse raced and my other organs made their own arrangements. The next week, we were all agog at the imminent arrival of the legend. I had become friendly with one of the American writers on Marty's show, called Barr, so I had no trouble remembering his name, even in the later stages of the evening. He was one of the few Americans who loved the bar: even then, mineral water was *de rigueur* among our visitors. I now realise that this must have been Barry Levinson, who went on to fame as a Hollywood director. If it wasn't, sorry Barry, and warm greetings to whoever it was.

Standing with him at the bar one lunchtime, he pointed out a figure at a table in the restaurant. Sitting with Larry Gelbart, the producer of the show, was a stooped figure with glasses, a (real) moustache, and wearing a beret. It was him. I had brought with me, every day, a copy of *The Groucho Marx Letters*, a collection of his correspondence with TS Eliot, among others, on the off chance that he might sign it. Barry offered to take it over to him. 'He's having his lunch,' I protested, but Barry took the book over.

I watched him speak to Groucho, who peered across at me and then, with a quavering hand, signed the title page. Barry brought it back to me.

'What did he put?' I asked.

'I didn't look,' he said.

I showed him the page. It bore the legend: 'From Groucho'.

'Don't you want it personalised?' said Barry, and before I could stop him he went back again with the book. I winced and tried to make myself invisible. Groucho again looked in my direction and duly wrote again. Barry brought the book back.

'I asked him to put "To Barry",' said my namesake, and, to add insult to injury, had also requested him to append 'Marx'. How many Grouchos are there, for God's sake? By now somewhat confused, Groucho had put 'Marx' next to my name by mistake and was corrected by Barry. So I now own a copy of the letters with the dedication: 'To Barry Marx from Groucho Marx'. He treated me like a brother.

The heart-breaking part of the whole experience was that Groucho, by then old and frail, was having trouble with the lines for the show, which had to be written on cards for him and were then delivered in short sections, stopping recording each time, and his voice had become faint. No matter how he was miked, the song he also did on the show was not picked up well enough to satisfy the sound man.

It was rather like meeting Muhammad Ali in later years. But the joy is that we don't have to rely on memories any more: the Grouchos of this world are alive and well, in full cry on tape and film.

I did meet him later that week and we chatted. Two things I remember from our conversation. Both were sad, but said in that inimitable voice they sounded almost funny. Looking at his watch, he said, 'Where's my car? Don't they know I haven't long for this world?' When we were discussing swimming, for some reason, he mentioned his pool. 'You like swimming?' I asked. 'I do, but I don't,' he replied, enigmatically. 'They found a friend of mine floating in *his* pool,' he said. On a happier or, rather, different note, Groucho's daughter was refused entry to a club pool, the unstated, but obvious, reason being that she was Jewish. Groucho contacted the club. 'For your information, she's half Jewish; can't she go in up to her waist?' he asked.

What fascinated me was that, due to his age, his walk had literally become the bent-kneed lope we all remember, and, whenever he passed a woman, he would give her the leer with the waggled eyebrows, almost as a reflex reaction.

Some years before, he had been in London to record an English version of his show *You Bet Your Life*, which Bill Cosby later revived. I am reminded of the moment in the American version when a contestant informed Groucho, the host, that he had thirteen children.

'Why you got thirteen children?' asked Groucho.

'Because I love my wife,' said the man.

'I love my cigar,' responded Groucho, 'but I take it out now and again.'

I saw Chico Marx at the Empire Theatre (there it is again) in the fifties. We couldn't believe it was actually him. The act was delightful, but what I remember most was his entrance, holding two grapefruit up to his chest.

'Jane Russell!' he beamed at the audience. That certainly carbon dates that moment.

I also saw Laurel and Hardy and the only parallel I can draw with today is a rock concert. The queue was round the block and the buzz was tangible. They were really here. The theatre was packed and when, at the end of the supporting bill, we suddenly heard the strains of 'The Dance of the Cuckoos' a roar went up. On they came, visibly older, as frail as Groucho, but unmistakably them. The ovation went on for some time and tears ran down Ollie's face. Stan just smiled. I don't remember, or even care, what they did that night; it was enough to see them. Correction, I remember Ollie bowing and allowing his bowler hat to fall on the stage. As he bent to pick it up, favouring the audience with the sight of his impressive rear, Stan kicked him. 'That'll teach you to show off,' he said. You had to be there.

BARRY CRYER – AN APPRECIATION

By David Nobbs
Additional Material by Barry Cryer

BARRY IS FAR too modest ever to boast of how modest he is. He describes himself as 'a bits and pieces man'. Ridiculous. What he means is that he's good at more things than the rest of us. This means that, in an era dominated by pigeon-holing, he isn't taken as seriously as he should be for any of his many achievements.

Together, Barry and I wrote sketches for 68 editions of *Sez Les* (just missed 69, the story of my life). His fertility of ideas and knowledge of show biz was more than matched by his feeling for, and love of, words. He is an immaculate writer.

Writer, performer, quiz master, after-dinner speaker, drinking companion, ostrich trainer – Barry Cryer is all of these, and more. But I would say that his greatest gift is one of the rarest gifts of all: eyes light up and spirits lift when he enters a room. Knowing him is a joy.

SEVENTEEN

THE SKIN GAME

I MAKE NO apology for mentioning that I suffered from severe eczema through the years, particularly in my late teens and early twenties. This had reached an absolute peak in my early days in our business. You can imagine that the combination of bad skin and make-up was not a happy one.

One bizarre experience springs to mind. I was on tour in a comedy musical *The Quiz Kid*, inspired by the rash (unfortunate choice of word) of game shows then on television. Has nothing changed? My skin condition deteriorated and I had to leave the show in Glasgow and make my miserable journey home to Leeds. There I attended Leeds General Infirmary as an outpatient. I was covered from head to foot in bandaging, complete with white gloves and dark glasses. Got the picture? The invisible man.

One day as I emerged from hospital I decided not to get my usual taxi, but walk round Leeds as an experiment. I had remembered reading about Jose Ferrer, who, while filming *Cyrano de Bergerac*, had walked round Los Angeles wearing his Cyrano nose, to see people react. So I strolled through the shopping crowds and, indeed, I could have been invisible. I never saw anyone looking at me, although I did spot a mother remonstrating with a child. I went into a shop to buy cigarettes and the woman behind the counter, after a fractional hesitation, merely remarked about the hot weather.

What this proves I'm not quite sure, apart from the innate consideration of most people. As a schoolboy, I had penned an angry and extremely pompous letter to *The Goon Show* after they had done a joke about eczema. I received a reply from the producer, requesting I retain my sense of humour. I did, but I also retained my eczema. It didn't stop me listening to *The Goon Show*, and later I worked with Spike Milligan, Peter Sellers, Michael Bentine and Harry Secombe and, funnily enough, I never mentioned the letter.

Eczema, understandably, falls into the category of minor ailments to anyone who has not suffered, or known anyone who has, but, if you have been taken into hospital on a stretcher, which I was, more than once, or been in a ward where a fellow patient committed suicide because of the misery of the condition, 'minor' doesn't seem to be the word any more.

Because of that, I gladly made a video for the Eczema Society and I hope I've done my bit to try to educate people in the physical and psychological effects of this very common complaint. End of sermon. My eczema started to lessen after my marriage and has now virtually disappeared. Coincidence? Who knows. What I do know is that they still have not found a cure.

EIGHTEEN

GOON BUT NOT FORGOTTEN

MENTION OF SPIKE Milligan reminds me of one or two incidents when in the company of the guru of *Goon*. I once appeared on a radio quiz with him and we were paired as a team. After introducing us, the chairman went on to introduce the first member of the opposing team. After he had said the name, Spike leapt to his feet, crying, 'You mean the coffin was empty?'

Joe Brown, the singer, told me he once visited Spike's house and, while waiting for him to make an appearance, Joe's eye was taken to a very large and stark picture of the crucifixion. Joe moved nearer to have a closer look. Then he noticed, in the bottom right-hand corner in ballpoint, the dedication: 'To Spike'.

I did a TV show with Spike and, when I entered the hospitality room before the recording, Spike leapt to his feet (it seemed to have been one of his favourite occupations in those days) and went to the wall, spread his legs and leant against it, in police arrest fashion, and said, 'Cryer's here! Don't hurt me! Just take my jokes! Don't hurt me!'

When we appeared on the Kenny Everett show, he noticed that Ev had Autocue on every camera. He never learnt the lines in advance, but was a master at picking up the words quickly. Spike spotted this and said,

'Everett, I've learnt all my * * * *ing lines – remind me to send you an assassin for Christmas.'

I learnt all I know from Spike. Unfortunately, I didn't learn all *he* knows.

NINETEEN

THE GOOD COMPANION

SITTING ONE DAY with Graham Chapman after an especially warm lunch, I mentioned the name JB Priestley. 'I'm sick of you talking about him,' said Graham.

'Why?' I queried.

He told me that my obsession with Priestley, as he called it, was beginning to bore him and I should do something about it.

'Like what?' I said.

'Ring him,' said Graham.

'You can't just ring someone like that,' I protested.

'Why not?' he said.

Fifteen love. I remember my friend Wendy at YTV, who had made a documentary with JB, and rang her. She furnished me with his phone number. I dialled.

A woman answered.

Still glowing from lunch, I said, 'Is Mr Priestley in?'

No response; just a click.

'Hello?' he said. It was him. I sobered up immediately.

'My name's Barry Cryer,' I said.

'Is it indeed?' he replied. Fair enough.

My brain went into overdrive. 'Er . . . my mate and I . . .' I said (what could I say that would not worry him?), 'would like to have tea with you.'

'You're bloody mad. Where are you speaking from?' he said.

'London,' I replied.

'You'd come down here?' he asked.

'Yes,' I answered.

'Now I know you're mad. Who's your mate?' he asked.

'Graham Chapman – *Monty Python*,' I said.

'And you are?' he asked.

'Barry Cryer. I'm a writer,' I replied.

'I've heard you on the wireless,' he said.

My god knew of my existence: I floated on a pink cloud.

'We can't get *Monty Python* here,' JB said. The Priestleys lived in Alveston near Stratford on Avon, and the show had been taken off in the area. It wasn't networked by the BBC; in fact, if showjumping was on it would be relegated to after eleven o'clock at night. That sort of cavalier treatment rather suggested that the BBC were not aware that they had a hit on their hands.

'Three o'clock on Monday all right? I'm giving up my walk for you,' he said.

'Thank you,' I replied.

A click.

I looked at Graham and said, 'Tea on Monday.'

'Excellent,' Graham said.

I'd assumed that Priestley would be surrounded by secretaries, but I later found out that the woman who answered the phone was the cleaner.

We realised that the following Sunday *Monty Python* were to perform their first show at the Belgrade Theatre, Coventry, not a million miles from Stratford, and I was coming up to see it. Suddenly, the pieces fell into place. We booked a car to drive us to Alveston. John Cleese heard about the jaunt and decided to join us.

The show on Sunday night was a riot, with the circle full of Gumbys, Michael Palin's character with the knotted handkerchief on the head and the boots. Notwithstanding this alarming cult manifestation, the lads (lads?!) couldn't have wished for a better reception.

Monday morning dawned and we assembled. We drove down to Kissing Tree House, Alveston, a beautiful Georgian pile, and went up the drive to the front door. The cleaner ushered us in. Ahead of us stretched a marble hall and we walked down it to a door. We were shown into the library. The man himself rose to greet us.

Smaller than I'd expected, but, otherwise, the bulldog head and the pipe reminded you of every photograph you'd ever seen of JB. Within minutes, Graham and he were chatting about pipe tobacco (Graham smoked a pipe, among other things), and tea and cucumber sandwiches were served. With no sense of strain, the conversation flowed and flowed.

JB played the gruff Yorkshireman to the hilt, but the twinkle belied it. He asked about us and we desperately tried not to make the conversation sound like an interview. After informing us that he'd put netting over the pond to keep the herons off the goldfish, he answered our questions with good humour.

He told us, with no sign of ego, that he had been fêted in Russia and America and then vilified in both countries as a capitalist lackey and a communist respectively. He recalled that, when he was named in his wife Jacquetta's divorce case, he was dubbed a dirty old man; and then, when he became a founder member of the Campaign for Nuclear Disarmament, he was transformed into a dirty, *silly* old man. The tabloids were alive and well even then.

On and on poured the stories and the names. JB had walked and worked with the greatest. He couldn't stand Bruce Forsyth, but loved Jan Leeming, the newsreader.

The bookcase opened. It had a door concealed by the shelves. His wife, Jacquetta, came in and greeted us. I was convinced she'd been hovering, listening to confirm that we were not from *This Is Your Life*, or *Candid Camera*, or anything equally worrying.

The rest of the sunlit afternoon passed in a happy haze and we left, with promises to keep in touch on both sides.

We did. We took JB to dinner at the Café Royal – I thought that felt right. We walked down Piccadilly from Albany, where he had a town flat. He was wearing his broad-brimmed hat and a cape, looking like the man in the Sandeman's Port adverts. An old waiter greeted him warmly and said, 'Nice to see you again, Mr Priestley.' JB told me later that he hadn't been there for over twenty years.

On another occasion, JB entertained us in the flat and my wife and I went down to Alveston to have dinner with the Priestleys. After the meal, we watched *Some Like it Hot*, which he loved, accompanied by Billy Wilder stories, and then came the late-night news, read by Jan Leeming. JB padded over to the set and kissed the screen. He was an inveterate letter writer and always replied, always with some fascinating insight or reminiscence connected with something in your letter to him.

When JB died, I could honestly say I'd lost a friend, albeit one of only a few years' standing. We kept in touch with Jacquetta until she left to join him.

Meeting an idol can be dangerous and disappointing. You might find out they're only human, after all. JB was no disappointment: gruff and kindly, caustic and sentimental, but no sufferer of fools. He rebuked me at the Café Royal when my questions veered into chat-show mode.

Born as I was in Leeds, I'm familiar with emotions kept firmly under control by understatement. Jack had brought it to a fine art: he was angry at, and scornful of, many things, but his thoughts were invariably delivered calmly, with anger bubbling underneath. On the other hand, his enthusiasm and praise were straight from the shoulder, and he could be an unabashed fan. John Cleese, for instance, he said, should play Malvolio, and he'd always wanted Tony Hancock to play Ormonroyd, the photographer in *When We Are Married*.

Talking of *When We Are Married* (here he goes again), there was one of many revivals in the seventies, with Fred Emney playing the lenseman. Emney, with whom I had worked on *Jokers Wild*, was an enormous man with a monocle and cigar. He had been a big star, in every sense, in musical comedy and revues. He has also spent some time in Hollywood. I couldn't have enough of his company. JB, however, was none too happy with Fred's cavalier treatment of some of the lines in the play, but that was Fred.

One night, while sitting with the actress playing the maid, Fred forgot his lines. She leant over and whispered them to him. 'No, no,' boomed Fred, 'I say that.'

Rising from the settee, an impressive sight in itself, involving a certain amount of rocking to and fro, he finally achieved a vertical position. He looked at the maid. 'Did you feel the room move?'

He was the originator of one of the funniest, and yet strangely logical, lines I've ever heard about writing. At the dress rehearsals of *When We Are Married*, the only members of the audience were JB and the director. At the end, the curtain naturally didn't fall and the cast stood there like Madame Tussaud's. For reasons that were later explained, JB and the director got up and walked out. From the stage came Fred Emney's voice: 'If he didn't like it, he shouldn't have written it.'

While on the subject of things said about writing, someone who had watched a comedy about a scriptwriter entitled *Don't Forget to Write* by Charles Wood told me how much he'd enjoyed it, due to the obvious knowledge of the subject it contained. 'It must have been written by a writer,' he said. Think about that for a moment.

TWENTY

MAX TO THE WALL

I HAD ADMIRED Max Wall since I heard him as a boy (me, not him) on the radio in the forties and fifties. The warm, brown tones and the eccentric intonation grabbed my attention even then, 'Lashings of toast, simply o-o-oozing with butter.' In his act, he could make the word 'stool' sound as if it had four syllables. When I was working as a stagehand (all together now) at the Empire Theatre, Leeds, I watched from the wings, twice a night, as this grotesque figure, looking like Lon Chaney Senior in the silent *Phantom of the Opera*, cavorted and marched across the stage, with legs encased in obscene black tights and a rear view that defied description. I wanted to be him.

Later (I must stop saying that, but things that happen subsequently do tend to be 'later'), I got to know him. After a disastrous slump in his career, when he went out of fashion and, to compound the offence, left his wife and five children for a beauty queen, he made a triumphant comeback. He became an established actor and, among other plays, appeared in *Krapp's Last Tape* by Samuel Beckett. In this, he discovered the word 'spool', which he relished and, of course, invested with four syllables.

Entering a pub one evening, (oh, come on, a change is as good as a rest), I came upon Max, sitting in a corner with a pint of Guinness and a cheese sandwich. Calling for the wine list, I joined him. I asked how the play was going. He suddenly became philosophical and said, 'I spent forty years naked and alone, writing and stealing jokes, directing myself, and now I'm in a play. The fellow that's written the words is quite good;

I've got a man telling me what to do and there are other people involved, so it's not all my fault. It's a piece of piss.'

He didn't really mean it and yet, you know, in a very real sense, I think he did. He would say, 'I give them face 34 (he was renowned for his amazing range of facial expressions) and they call me a genius.' Cynical, yes; bitter, no. He was loving his born-again status.

One final memory. Ronnie Corbett told me, while he was working in Birmingham, that he noticed that Max was appearing in a small club on the outskirts. He made the pilgrimage to see him. The audience was barely in double figures and the great comic went through his paces to very little reaction. He suddenly looked at the audience and a wide, contented smile spread over his face. 'Do you know,' he said, 'this is the most restful part of my day?'

TWENTY-ONE

ACE KING JACK

I WORKED WITH Jack Benny in the seventies. He was in the twilight of an amazing career and it was like watching a masterclass. He had honed and refined his character, the conceited mean man, over decades, and you became convinced he had actually invented timing. In fact, Harold Pinter is reputed to have said he learnt the power of pauses from watching him.

I once watched him go through a script with a well-known comedian, indicating to the director where the camera shots should be. It dawned on us all that most of them should be on him, as his reactions would be where the comedy lay, not the comedian's lines. It was all done with such courtesy and grace that the comedian didn't notice that he had, to all intents and purposes, been removed from the sketch. Benny was, of course, right. It wasn't arrogance or pure ego, but judgment, a totally different thing altogether.

The morning after the recording, he recorded an insert for the show. It was a short piece that had been omitted the night before due to lack of recording time. There was obviously no audience in the studio that morning, just Jack and a camera. He delivered the lines as immaculately as ever, but with some mysterious pauses in the middle of sentences. He went into a booth with the sound engineer, who was going to dub on some laughs – a process we all hate but, on this occasion, unavoidable.

They played the tape back and Jack indicated where he wanted the laughs. A lesser comic would have merely wanted them after each joke, but not the Menuhin of mirth: 'No, not a big laugh there, it's not a great joke . . . Now, here where I've paused: put a laugh in there; they've just realised what I'm talking about.' It was enthralling. When the piece was edited into the show, you couldn't see the join. You would have sworn it was done on the night, in front of an audience. When you work with someone that good, you'd pay for the privilege. I will, of course, deny ever having said that.

The last time I saw him, I stood in the wings at the Palladium, on the night of what was to be Jack's last appearance in London. He walked down to the side of the stage, greeted me and waited to go on. His walk was slow and his shoulders were bowed. He was old and ill. The music played; the shoulders went back and all frailty disappeared. He walked on to tumultuous applause. The show must go on. Yes, it's a cliché. But never forget that clichés are the oysters in which we find the pearls of perception. I'll wait, while you write that one down. Or not.

TWENTY-TWO

TWO OF A KIND

WHEN I CAME to London, one of the first shows I went to see was Emlyn Williams' reading from Dickens. I say 'reading', but he'd learnt the whole thing and every five minutes or so would turn a page as a shared joke with the audience.

Williams was an interesting man, actor, writer, director and, allegedly, naughty boy. This was advanced as the reason why he never got a well-deserved knighthood. If actors deserve knighthood, that is. I always remember a fellow writer reminding me that the basis of our business was enter-taining the crowd while the pickpockets went round the back. We're basically rogues and vagabonds and should remain so. But don't get me on the subject of honours and who, if anyone, should receive them. Rather, read my book *Honour and Offer – The Trauma of Titles*, Maxwell Desktop Publications (remaindered).

Meanwhile, back at Emlyn Williams. He entered, costumed and bearded, and made his way to a lectern, on which was a large book, a carafe of water and a glass. He removed his gloves and began. (I once wrote a parody of this for Tommy Cooper, in which Tom removed his gloves and then his beard, but that's another story.) Playing all the characters, Emlyn evoked Dickens' world before our eyes and ears and I was enthralled. Soon after, I went to see his one-man *Bleak House*, which was equally impressive.

I wrote him a fan letter and three days later I received a hand-written reply, thanking me for taking the trouble to write to him. I know of only three other people who have done this: Alec Guinness, Victor Borge and Alan Bennett. I hasten to add that they represent three of the few people I have written to; you're not looking at an autograph anorak. Although I still treasure the signed McDonalds serviette from Keith Chegwin.

I saw Williams' Dylan Thomas show and his perform-ance of Saki short stories, but we never met until years later, when I was in a charity show at the Shaftesbury Theatre in London. As is usually the case on these occasions, a dozen of us were sharing a large dressing room. Ronnie Stevens, the actor, who knew of my admiration for Williams, pointed to a small, white-haired figure in the corner. 'There he is,' said Ronnie.

Brash as ever, I approached and introduced myself.

'Sit down,' Williams said.

He pretended, charmingly, to remember my letter of years before and, once again, an idol did not crumble. I looked at my watch.

'We'd better get ready,' I said.

'True,' he replied, and dropped his trousers and then his pants. He requested I stay as he changed. Not only had I met my idol, but had seen him as nature intended. Ronnie Stevens later described this as 'a discreet flash'. No matter, to me he was idol intacta.

Victor Borge also wrote back to me and I subsequently did the warm-up for one of his TV shows. Having warmed up for him and Noël Coward, I can only marvel at my hubris. ('Hubris' means partner of 'Nemesis', and what an act they were.)

In my defence, I had realised that telling jokes before introducing someone of Borge's stature was not to be advised. So I obtained his biography from his agent and related it to the audience. So far, so good. Then, as happened on the Noël Coward night, a malign fate decreed that there would be a technical hold-up. I talked on and on and then, to my relief, got the signal to bring him on. 'And now, the reason you're all here tonight: Mr Victor Borge!' He walked on, gave me a gracious nod and the show began.

A few minutes later and we stopped again. The floor manager hissed at me, 'Get on.'

'I'm not telling jokes,' I bleated.

'You're being paid,' he said.

Unanswerable. I went on and began to talk, yet again, for what seemed to be an eternity while the problem was being sorted out. I finally capitulated and told some jokes.

From the corner of my eye, I could see Mr Borge standing on the side, watching me. My spirits sank. Yet again, I got the signal and, yet again, I introduced him. Yet again, he walked on. I moved out of the spotlight, bowing obsequiously. He seized my arm in a vicelike grip. Oh God, what was he going to say?

'Ladies and gentlemen,' he said, 'now you know why I'm here: to fill in the gaps between Barry Cryer.' Ah well.

We met again at a Variety Club lunch in his honour. He spoke with his customary deadpan mastery and he was then asked to play the piano, which was on the other side of the room. The chief barker told him he would keep talking, to enable Victor to make his way over to the piano. 'Good,' said Victor, 'I'll stay here and listen to you.'

Only someone whose first language was not English (he was born in Denmark) could have used it in such an imaginative way. I once heard him interviewed on the radio. A name was mentioned.

The interviewer said, 'Is he still alive?'

'No,' said Victor, 'he's still dead.'

'You come from Copenhagen?' the interviewer asked.

'All the time,' said Victor.

TWENTY-THREE

FROST IN ALL AREAS

My LIFE HAS, let's face it, been a series of lucky accidents. I wrote for a revue at the Fortune Theatre and Danny La Rue came in one night. He asked me to write his nightclub shows. David Frost came to the club one night and asked me to write for him. What I did to deserve these breaks is still not clear to me. But enough of paralysis by analysis.

David told me he'd seen me at the Players' Theatre and asked me to do warm-ups for his shows as well as writing. At first I demurred, but he persisted. So, with my usual decision to frighten myself, I agreed. Thus began years of plying my trade as a warm-up man.

It's the toughest job in television. You're the human Polyfilla between the recorded scenes, the link with the audience. It's pointless doing an act: you never know how long you have got anyway, and you look as if you're auditioning or trying to compete with the show. I know quite a few warm-up men – it's invariably a male occupation – who have become, shall we say, a trifle bitter, due to the fact that, when the camera goes on, they go off. But I always enjoyed it.

It's indefinable. You talk, not knowing when you'll finish, and an insensitive floor manager may well interrupt you in the middle of a joke, or suddenly throw you into the arena to fill in.

The *Pythons* once recorded a TV special called 'How to Irritate People', a title that John Cleese said was highly appropriate as the recording lasted some three hours. Guess who was the warm-up man. I think I went on seventeen times that night and they bore me off to the bar afterward, Michael Palin commenting, 'You were on more than we were.' Towards the end, I was reduced to talking about my children, my health and, at one point, real tennis and corn circles. The long day's journey into the night is the lot of the warm-up man and many of us have white hair as a result.

David Frost left the BBC after *The Frost Report* and went to ITV; first Rediffusion and then London Weekend Television. I went with him as jobbing writer and warm-up man. We did three shows a week and after a day's writing I would clock on for warm-up duty. I should point out that the shows were live and much sought after by warm-up practitioners, as you only had to go on at the beginning and during the commercial break. David had a playful habit of arriving in the studio at the last minute – something to do with keeping his adrenaline count high. One night he walked in as I was still talking and the credits were about to roll. As he walked onto the set,

I dived flat on the floor and was hauled off under the camera by one of the crew.

One night, he opened the show and then immediately dashed up the road to Wembley Arena to play a quick burst of tennis with Lew Hoad. The theory was that there would be two or three items one after the other in the show and then he would return. This was live, I must remind you. I was asked to sit in his chair just in case he didn't make it. He assured me he would. He didn't.

'The wonderful Julie Felix!' I back-announced, trying desperately not to do the Frost impression all we writers had perfected. I went on to introduce the next item. David rushed in, furious at having failed his own challenge. Oh, those nights with Frost, as Michael Fish once said.

Then there was the night when Emil Savundra, who ran an insurance company that had decamped with clients' money, was nearly lynched by the studio audience. There was Dr Petro, a doctor and drug dealer, who was staked out by the police and arrested as he left the studio. The night of the Yippies (who?), an alternative-lifestyle group, who cheerfully insulted David and sprayed everyone with water pistols. In the ensuing chaos, David announced that the second half of the show would be in a different studio. Sure enough, come the second half, there were David and the author, Robert Ardrey, in a deserted studio with one camera. Shock, horror!

Footnote: You can't just go into another studio at a

moment's notice and find everything ready for you to transmit a programme. Surely I'm not suggesting that the whole thing was set up in advance? Perish the thought. Second footnote: Jerry Rubin, leader of the Yippies, became incredibly rich and a pillar of Wall Street.

TWENTY-FOUR

LES MAJESTY

WHAT CAN ONE say about Les Dawson that he wouldn't interrupt? We had a long professional relationship, both in *Jokers Wild* and his own shows. A word about *Jokers Wild*.

It was devised by Ray Cameron (see the Kenny Everett show) and Mike King, of the King brothers, my friend from way back. 'Inspired' by an American radio show called *Can You Top That?*, the format was simplicity itself. Six comedians, myself as chairman, told jokes and interrupted each other. That's it.

I was recently sent a video of some of the early shows and was surprised by two things. First, I had black hair; and second, everybody seemed to be smoking. I had an ashtray in front of me and the whole show was wreathed in smoke. Now, of course, smokers are social lepers and I deeply resent being asked to go outside if I want a cigarette. Whatever the pilot says.

Les was a mainstay of *Jokers Wild*. In fact, Michael Aspel described doing the show as taking a train to Leeds to listen to Les. Other regulars in the early days included Ted Ray and Arthur Askey, two giants of variety from the thirties through to the fifties and still going strong in the seventies. All of us had great respect for those veterans and they were full of received wisdom and anecdotes. Arthur once gave me the best definition of our – or, indeed, anybody's – business. He said, 'Every generation's the same. A load of crap and a few brilliant people.'

I always remember this when I hear people of my generation knocking the new breed of comedians. They usually haven't seen many, but dismiss them as 'dirty jeans and saying fuck all the time'. Not so. They really should get out more and see what's happening. Eddie Izzard, to name but one, is as funny as anyone I remember. So there.

What was I talking about? Oh yes, Les. After a tough apprenticeship ('I was a flop during the boom'), he made an appearance on *Opportunity Knocks* and that was the breakthrough. Lugubrious and with an abiding love of words for their own sake, he was much admired by other comics. He was a throwback to stars of yore like Robb Wilton, Norman Evans and Frank Randle, whose styles could be discerned in his work. Someone said that originality was undetected plagiarism, but Les was more than just an amalgam of previous comics. There was something there that was uniquely him. In a word, 'doom'. Every silver lining had its concomitant cloud.

On one of the *Joker's Wild* shows, Jack Douglas, the *Carry On* team member, told a long, rambling story about eternity, comparing it to waiting for Les to buy a round. Les walked off the set, while the cameras were rolling, and made his way to the bar. The rest of us filled in. He returned, bearing a tray, on which were drinks for everyone except Jack.

Les had several series on YTV: *Sez Les, Les Sez* and other ingenious permutations. I wrote with David Nobbs and Peter Vincent, both old friends from previous campaigns. The stalwart Roy Barraclough appeared in most of them and, looking back, I hope with an unsentimental eye, they still seem funny.

Les as the incompetent stunt man, Buster Gutt; Les as Jock Cousteau, the underwater piper (in a real water tank); Les, as Count Otto Von Death, the wrestler, done in a ring, with the studio audience as the crowd; Les and John Cleese, who appeared in several shows as Foreign Legionnaires and First World War pilots (Les's agent, Norman Murray, remarked that he thought John Cleese was quite funny); Les playing the grand piano, suspended in midair on wires; and, of course, Les as Cosmo Smallpiece, the sex-crazed television presenter. Les and Roy as Cissie and Ada, or was it the other way round? Who cares. It was glorious.

After several happy years in Leeds, Les was presented with a plaque, wrapped in newspaper ('They could at least have made it today's paper,' he said), and he left for the BBC.

A portent of Kenny Everett, years later: the BBC never knew what to do with Les. They didn't even trust him to star in his own show, teaming him with Lulu. After various experiments, he took over from Terry Wogan on *Blankety Blank*. That was as near as his employers ever got to the real Les. Terry had cheerfully offered himself up as a butt for the panel's jokes – the selfless straight man; but Les went in, all guns blazing, insulting panellists, prizes and the producer relentlessly. It worked, but it still wasn't, in a true sense, the Les Dawson show. I never cease to marvel at people who sign artists because of their success elsewhere and then have no idea what to do with them. Surely I don't mean that such people don't justify the positions they hold? Surely not.

Les, unlike most comedians, was exactly the same offstage as on, and I'm convinced that the constant strain of performing, each and every day, wherever he was, hastened his death. A confirmed people-aholic, he was always on show and never seemed to relax. I miss him.

TWENTY-FIVE

WELCOME TO MORECAMBE

THE LATE BERNIE Winters, half of a double act with his brother, Mike, said of Morecambe and Wise, 'An act like them occurs once in a lifetime. Why did they have to happen in ours?' Typically generous and, of course, true.

I first met Eric and Ernie when they were in variety and making their way up the bill. Eric used to say that those were the happy days, when they didn't have the responsibility of being stars and they could steal the show.

They were, in those days, self-confessed admirers of Abbott and Costello and, in fact, Ernie used to slap *Eric's* face. But their own style was evolving.

I stood on the side of the stage at the old ABC Theatre in Blackpool and watched as they came off from doing their act at the end of the show. All they had to do was rush upstage, up some stairs and then walk down for the finale. But waiting in the wings was Eric's dresser, with a cigarette. Two quick puffs and onward.

Later, of course, he had to give up, due to his heart

problems. He used to suck on an empty pipe or treat himself
to a forbidden cigar.

I wrote for them with John Junkin, Mike Craig, Lawrie
Kinsley and Ron McDonnell through the years, always aware
that Eddie Braben, who had come to them from Ken Dodd
(rumour had it, he dug a big tunnel), was the A team. And
I must mention Sid Green and Dick Hills, who wrote their
ITV shows and first made them stars. I once said to Eric,
'Sid and Dick made you stars; Eddie made you an institu-
tion; and we'll make you has-beens.' How he laughed.

Eric and Ernie, after their memorable success at the BBC,
signed for Thames. The Kenny Everett story in reverse. Yet
again, cries of 'Betrayal!', 'Disloyalty!' I always distrust the
word 'loyalty' when used by employers. I'm sorry, but it's the
way I am. That, coupled with the personal experience.

John Junkin and I were hired to write for them, as Eddie
Braben was still under contract to the BBC. We had a happy
time, penning, among other epics, 'Jekyll and Hyde' with
Judi Dench and 'Butler of the Year' with Donald Sinden,
and a whole ream of sketches and songs. But we were always
haunted by the constant theme: 'Not as funny as they were
at the BBC.' It's a point of view, but not, in my unbiased
opinion, true. I *am* unbiased, as a matter of fact, having
written for them on both sides of the fence.

The working schedule at Thames was a mere two shows
a year, in stark contrast to the old weekly grind that Eric
said was 'all done on fear'. This more relaxed mode was to

make sure Eric didn't overtax himself, but it gave us more time to discuss and write shows and then more time to discard them. We finished up, after three drafts, writing a Christmas show based on ideas by Eric that was not an unqualified success. John and I decided to resign in order to give them a chance to break in new writers or wait for Eddie, who was coming to the end of his BBC contract.

We took them out to lunch. They were intrigued. Writers taking stars to lunch? By the brandy stage, John and I looked at each other. It was time. 'What a lovely way of handing in our resignation,' said John.

Eric said, 'Is that a joke?'

We assured them it wasn't. I said that the show hadn't worked. It would, understandably, be regarded as our fault, not theirs. They were Morecambe and Wise.

Ernie pondered, smiled and said, 'Do you mean we can be as bad a we like?'

We did, in fact, write for them again, but the great days were over. But I will never forget the pleasure of writing for them, secure in the knowledge that your stuff was going to get maximum value in performance.

Eric was the quickest brain I have ever worked with. A case in point. He was usually word perfect and rarely fluffed a line. But, on one show, while talking about BBC bosses, he said to Ernie, 'Oh yes, there they are, walking down the powers of corridor.'

Ernie looked at him. 'Pardon?' he asked.

'Backwards, of course,' said Eric.

During the making of one of the Thames shows, we were all assembled in an office in Euston Road. The room was filled with all the people associated with a show: designers, sound, lighting, producer et al. All the usual suspects. I began to detect what I later described as Latin American rhythms in my heartbeat − a sense of missing the beat about three times a minute. Eric noticed my alarm. 'What's the matter?' he asked.

'Barry's heart,' said John.

'Get the nurse,' said Eric.

I was lucky enough to be in the presence of an expert on the subject. I lay on the floor, which, in retrospect, is the worst thing you can do.

The nurse sat me up and did the usual tests. I was rushed over the road to University College Hospital. There I had an X-ray, an electrocardiogram and a complete check-up. I awaited the verdict. The doctor looked at the results, asked if I smoked, took my pack of cigarettes, screwed them up and threw them in the bin.

'You don't deserve it, but you're fine,' he said.

Thames offered me a car home, but I declined and went out into the sunshine, whistling and saying hello to strangers. I entered the office and reassured the throng that I was all right and that the Grim Reaper had postponed. Eric took me to one side.

'I must tell you what happened while you were away,' he

said. 'We were talking about you and wondering how you were getting on and Ernie was reading the script,' he continued.

Then, he told me that Ernie suddenly looked up and said, 'I know what's wrong.' They looked at him. 'We come on too late in this sketch,' he said.

Eric never let me forget it. If you're reading this, Ern, I forgive you. It's nothing compared to the pleasure it all was.

Two final memories of Eric. There was a big awards show at the Palladium, hosted by David Frost. At one point, Eric and Ernie came up to receive their latest award. During the unscripted conversation on the stage, Eric looked at David. 'Are you in New York *now*?' he asked. The best definition of David I've ever heard. With the possible exception of Eric Idle's capsule definition of David: 'And now – germ warfare. Ted Ray – any thoughts?'

Eric was once cornered by a man who was feeling no pain at a party. The tired and emotional one started pontificating about show business, to Morecambe, of all people. Reaching a climax, he said, 'I always think, to be in show business, you need three things.'

'If you've got three things, you should be in the circus,' said Eric.

There's no answer to that – somewhere glasses are being raised and waggled.

TWENTY-SIX

STAND UP AND BE COUNTED

I'VE ALREADY REFERRED to the fact that I can't stand people pronouncing on young performers, or indeed, anything, sight unseen. For over thirty years I wrote jokes, sketches and sitcoms. And, more to the point, topical jokes: on the Frost shows, we were still writing them on that day. So I assume that helped me to roll along with each succeeding generation, instead of becoming some poor old sexist and racist comic, sitting in the corner, enthusing over the old and damning the new. Right. Having established what a wonderful, tolerant, open-minded and *young at heart* person I am, may I continue? (You do what you like, Baz; we're losing the will to live.)

But, seriously(!), having worked alongside everyone from Max Miller to Rory Bremner and Clive Anderson, I hope I'm still receptive to what's happening.

I met Ben Elton in the gents at Central Television and we started talking, as you do. We were both there to appear in their live Friday-night programme, which specialised in confrontation. An employee of Central was standing close by, as you do, and said, 'Excuse me, you two know you're being stitched up tonight, don't you?' We didn't and he proceeded to mark our cards. The subtext of the show was to be 'The Battle of the Comics' and the premise was 'old' versus 'new'. How do they think of these things? And why?

The 'old' were myself, Michael Bentine and my friend, Neil Shand, a colleague from the Frost days. The 'new' were Ben Elton, John Lloyd (producer of *Spitting Image*, *Blackadder* and *Not the Nine O'Clock News*) and Stephen Fry. We met in the green room and conferred. We decided we would be the stitchers, not the stitchees.

The show was fronted by a woman whose name I shall mercifully withhold – mainly because I can't remember it – and she was clutching a clipboard. She laid down the rules of the conflict.

Ben, as I remember, opened the batting with a statement about the very nature of comedy.

'That is so true,' said Michael Bentine.

Neil made an observation.

'Oh yes, I agree,' said Stephen.

And so it went on, with everybody agreeing with everyone else.

At one point, Michael noticed that the studio floor had a picture of a roundel on it, the red, white and blue circular emblem that was on the side of our planes during the Second World War. He commented on this and then embarked on a wartime reminiscence involving the Battle of Britain.

I then cried, 'The Battle of the Comics!' and lay on the floor. I think at this point the woman discarded the clipboard.

During the series of *The Stand-up Show* on television and radio, I have met nothing but friendliness and cooperation from the young comics I have worked with. I've never noticed a generation gap. I'm Uncle Baz, and proud of it.

Mark Thomas, a fierce, polemical, brilliant comedian, invited me to join him at the Red Shoe Club in Seven Sisters Road in Holloway, after we had met in Edinburgh. Came the night and I joined him backstage. My nerve was failing rapidly. Mark said he'd introduce me and I stood on the side (another good title for this book), regretting the whole thing. Mark did some 25 minutes, reducing the audience to rubble and then, with a rather lavish comparison of me with Elvis, he introduced me. I walked on, wishing I was at home. A girl at the front went, 'Aaah.' It was like her dad had just come on. I had a very happy time and came off. Mark said that if I ever said 'fuck' on the stage he'd never speak to me again. Wise words.

What does it all mean? Simply that comedy is comedy. Topics and social norms may change, but funny is always funny. (Congregation murmuring 'How true' rises and sings 'knock knock' jokes to the tune of 'Jerusalem'.)

The esoteric world of after-dinner speaking takes up a lot of my time. It's a law unto itself. No two speakers are alike and many of the finest and funniest are not in my business. Beware the priest, the doctor, the lawyer, and even the accountant. If they have the humour to see their situation and the memory to recall the funny things that happened, they're in business.

David Nobbs recalls seeing a sober-suited man of a certain age stand up to speak. There was no noticeable *frisson* of anticipation from the audience as he looked, to put it delicately, rather grey and low-key. 'I must apologise if I seem tired,' he said. 'The postman woke me at six o'clock this morning. That's the last time I sleep with him,' he continued. The incongruity was brilliant. He went on to talk about his son, who narrowly missed a blue at Cambridge. It was nestling behind the pink.

Years ago I joined the Lord's Taverners. I'm not by nature a joiner; I'm more of a mixer, if you see what I mean. I think it was a direct result of an evening spent with Willie Rushton and Tim Brooke-Taylor, the details of which escape me. Anyway, I became Lord's Taverner number 1066.

That reminds me, as it would, of the story of King Harold inspecting his bowmen the night before the Battle of Hastings. Coming to the first archer, he commanded him to show him what he could do. The man shot an arrow and pinned a butterfly to a barn door.

'I'm cheering up,' said the king.

He arrived at the second bowman. This man threw a clod of earth up in the air and pierced it with three arrows.

'I'm feeling sanguine about the morrow,' said the king.

He came to the third man, who was leaning on his bow.

'Now, you,' said the king.

The man fired an arrow, which missed the barn door, ricocheted off a tree and was never seen again.

'Watch out for this one,' said the king, 'he'll have somebody's eye out in the morning.'

'What is the point of all of this!' you cry. Here it is. Soon after I joined the Taverners, they asked me to speak at their Christmas lunch at the Café Royal. Flattered, I agreed.

I mentioned this to Eric Morecambe, who said, 'You're mad. Why didn't you make them wait?'

I duly turned up and mingled with the throng, concealing my apprehension under a veneer of light banter and a lot of champagne. I was to follow Jim Laker, the former England bowler. Jim was recently out of hospital, following heart surgery. He was much admired and very funny. I sat listening to him in despair. Then I remembered something I'd read in a book, concerning this very situation, i.e. following a speaker who tears the place up. I was introduced. The sympathy of the audience at my plight was all to evident.

'Jim and I were chatting over lunch,' I said, 'and we thought it would be fun to swap speeches.'

That did the trick and I survived.

Afterward, a few people asked if I did after-dinner speaking, to which I replied, 'No.' That night, my wife suggested that in future I say yes and see what happened.

I started getting bookings and learning the trade. You're not doing an act as a speaker; the atmosphere is much more informal than that. You might (!) tell some jokes, but it's a case of same meat, different gravy. You dress the material differently. It's good to personalise your offering and mention some names right at the beginning that provide a vehicle for jokes. Not the people themselves – you are a guest and might break one or two eggshells if you're flippant about the managing director – but about their titles and interests.

Golf is always a safe bet, but golfers have heard all the golf jokes, so I usually just say, 'I don't play golf, I *like* women.' That stirs the water. While on the subject of in-house jokes relating to the business your audience is in, forget them. The jokes, not the audience. It's no good telling computer people computer jokes: they've heard them before. Builders know more and better jokes about their trade than you do, so relax.

Usually, the audience is warm and receptive, but, as ever, the horror stories are the ones that stick in the mind. I will never forget salesmen and -women in Guernsey. They were out of it even before dinner, due to redundancies and dramas that very day, that I knew not of. When I rose to speak, I was greeted with merry cries of 'W* * * * *!' and 'C* * *!' It's somewhat difficult to keep the boat afloat after a start like that. But, somewhere, there is a smile to be had, even on the darkest night. At one dinner, I had just started speaking when a languid voice at the back said, 'What do you do?'

'If you give me a chance, I'll show you,' I quipped.

I pressed on and a few minutes later the same voice said, 'I repeat, what do you do?'

I started a joke one night and a man, sitting at a front table, said loudly, 'Oh, I like this one.' On an impulse, I invited him to join me and we told the story as a double act. I engineered it so that he got the punchline, so I hoped I would finish up in the role of Mr Nice Guy.

Willie Rushton once spoke to twelve young denizens of the futures market in the City and while he was speaking one of them mounted the table, did an impression of a horse breaking wind and then sang a song. Willie said good night and left, which I think was a reasonable response under the circumstances.

My own record for the smallest audience I spoke to was ten, and it presents quite a challenge. I mention that Willie and I did our act to ten thousand people at the Docklands Arena. If half of them laugh, it's a wonderful sound. If five out of ten laugh, it's not so exciting. I have actually declined to stand up with a small audience, as I'd met them all before dinner, so I just sat there, chatting. It's horses for courses. (Please make notes of these pearls of wisdom, if you so wish.)

The dinner scene spans everything from the Guildhall, complete with royalty and a toastmaster, to a knees-up with a merry crowd, straight from work, joyfully flashing their tattoos and hellbent on seducing each other. I once continued speaking while sitting on a woman's lap, where I had been placed by a very large man, with whom it was inadvisable to argue.

I've spoken on riverboats, swaying gently; cruise liners, rolling violently in the open air and high wind; hundreds of feet above London at a 'topping out' ceremony, after they'd finished the building; on a train; in a marquee during a gale; in an underground cave; and once in a restaurant when I turned up on the wrong night but they asked me to speak anyway.

I've sat listening to an attorney-general speaking so lengthily and boringly that someone said loudly, 'Oh God, I'm pleading guilty and going home.'

I've been asked to 'keep it clean' immediately before speaking to an audience that threw bread rolls at each other: a man was sick on the carpet in front of me and the police were called after a fight broke out. These Barbara Cartland fans are really something.

Basil Boothroyd, a courtly, charming man, told me that he once spoke to a Women's Institute audience that was incredibly mobile. While he was speaking, a woman rose from her seat and walked out. She later returned and another woman got up and left. This process was repeated throughout his performance. Afterwards, over tea with the chairperson, he commented on this.

'Oh yes,' she said, 'Wednesday's the chiropodist.'

I was once asked to continue speaking as we all moved from one room to another to witness a video display. A sort of walking commentary.

Willie once got up to speak at a lunch where I was present. He had been clearly visible throughout the meal, in conversation with Norman Tebbitt. 'I've just been talking to Tebbitt,' boomed Will. 'An experience rather akin to taking tea with the Krays,' he continued. It's a rich, many-coloured dreamcoat of a world.

John Betjeman was once requested, by letter, to deliver a talk on Reading. Being a keen student of architecture and the history of towns, he prepared a piece on Reading's outstanding features. He delivered this to an attentive, but baffled, audience. The were expecting him to talk about 'reading' (the verb).

TWENTY-SEVEN

MY FAVOURITE MARTIAN

I ALWAYS THOUGHT that Tommy Cooper looked like Mount Rushmore on legs. Together with Les Dawson and Ken Dodd, he seemed to prove JB Priestley's theory that great comics are alien visitors from another planet. Did you ever see anyone who looked exactly like Tommy in real life?

I wrote for Tom at Thames and London Weekend Television and it was an experience like no other. To say he was hard to write for is to understate the case. Enjoyable, yes, but difficult. Tom was essentially a great soloist. He had a problem remembering the cues for the other performers. So we had to find a repertory company of artists who could adapt to his meanderings and guide him back to the script. I always thought that the perfect Cooper sketch could be summarised as: 'Tom enters tailor's shop. Does tailoring jokes. Sketch ends.'

You could never predict how he would react in any given situation. There was a story about him buying a round of drinks. (This was not as rare an event as people allege. I was with him twice when he bought a round and I have the

Polaroids to prove it.) After handing round the drinks, he went to pick up his change from the bar. It had gone. People assured him he'd already taken it, but he wasn't convinced. The barman insisted that he'd given Tommy the money, but he still wasn't satisfied. Finally, he said to the barman, after a hunt under beer mats and behind the peanut bowl, 'You don't understand. It's not the principle of the thing; it's the money.'

We were rehearsing in St Paul's Church Hall in Hammersmith and Tom and I left to visit the Britannia pub opposite. It was opening time – a reminder of those quaint old days when pubs weren't open all day – and Tom bought me a drink. (No Polaroid of this incident exists.) A man approached Tom and punched his arm. 'Can I tell you a joke, Tommy?' he asked.

'Don't you know?' replied Tom, which I still think was the perfect response. I knew there and then something was going to happen. The punch had done it.

Undeterred, the man started: 'These two men go into a pub and . . .'

Tommy interrupted him: 'Sorry, sorry,' said Tommy. He turned to the barman and asked, 'Have you got a piece of paper?' The barman obliged. Tom smiled at the man and said, 'Sorry, carry on.'

'These two men went into . . .' continued the man.

Tom turned to the barman again. 'Have you got a pen? I can't find mine,' he said. A pen arrived. Tom smiled again, apologetically, and said, 'Sorry. Excuse me, have these men got names?'

'No, no . . . their names don't matter,' the man replied.

'Right,' said Tom, and duly wrote something on the piece of paper.

'So they . . .' the man said.

'Sorry. Is the name of the pub important? Or could it be any old pub?' Tommy asked.

'No, the pub doesn't need to have a . . .' the man answered.

'Sorry, go on,' said Tom, and wrote down 'Any old pub'.

The man doggedly attempted to tell the story, with Tom stopping him regularly to verify various details. Finally, the punchline was drawing near. It was obvious that Tom knew the joke. Just as the man was about to deliver the punchline, Tommy spotted one of the crew.

'Harry! Come and hear this joke!' he said, and turned to the man. 'Would you mind starting again? Harry's just got here,' Tommy said.

And with that he turned and walked out of the pub.

I was told the following story at Thames. The morning didn't exist for Tom. He'd spent his working life in theatres and clubs and was known to stay up half the night 'unwinding'. Then television discovered him, which meant he had to get up to go to rehearsals. Then he was introduced to the world of filming, which meant he had to rise even earlier.

The scene was the dining room of one of the Bourne-mouth hotels. It was 6.30 in the morning. Tom sat looking grey and not in the best of humours. A waitress approached him and asked him what he'd like for breakfast.

'I'd like a large gin and tonic and a bowl of cornflakes,' said Tom.

'The bar is closed, sir. It's half past six in the morning,' she replied, laughing nervously.

'The manager's a friend of mine,' said Tom. The waitress left.

Some five minutes later, she returned with a bowl of cornflakes, a bottle of tonic and a large gin. Tom poured the gin all over the cornflakes.

He smiled at her and said, 'Milk's full of cholesterol, you know that, don't you?'

It's impossible to convey that unique delivery in print, but you can probably hear that voice.

This is one of Tom's favourite jokes. A hyena and a gorilla were talking. The hyena said, 'I'm fed up.'

'Why's that?' asked the gorilla.

'Well, every morning, I go for a walk – a little constitutional [you should have heard him say that] and this lion keeps jumping out of the undergrowth and beating me up,' said the hyena.

'Oh dear, I don't like that,' said the gorilla.

'I'm not mad about it myself,' said the hyena.

'If I ever see that happen, I shall intervene on your behalf,' said the gorilla.

'Thank you,' said the hyena.

The next morning, the hyena went for his usual walk and, sure enough, the lion jumped out, beat him up and ran off. The hyena lay there, groaning, 'Oh, oh [agonised face and faint noises].' He looked up and saw the gorilla, relaxing nonchalantly on the branch of a tree. 'Excuse me,' said the hyena, 'you said if you saw that happening, you'd intervene on my behalf.'

'I did,' said the gorilla, 'but you were laughing so much I thought you were winning.'

In his club act, the band played Tom's signature tune, 'The Sheik of Araby', and the audience applauded enthusiastically. He didn't come on. Instead, his voice was heard: he was apparently locked in his dressing room. The laughs that resulted would have been the envy of any comedian who was actually on stage. There was quite a lot of this before he actually made his entrance, to renewed delight.

Eric Morecambe once said to me, 'That bugger just stands there and they laugh. I have to start working.' They were old friends and shared great mutual respect. Which reminds me – I was in the b*r of Thames Television . . . Now look, I'm a purely social drinker, all right? I never drink alone. Well, a goldfish is somebody, isn't it? I was in the comfort station and Tom walked in. I say 'walked in', but he actually paused in the doorway, until someone shouted, 'What are you having, Tom?'

'That's very kind of you,' he said.

We were chatting and he remarked that Eric and Ernie

were about to record a show downstairs in the studio. 'Let's pop in,' said Tom. We went to the studio. Eric and Ernie had just started their warm-up before the recording started. Tom moved unobtrusively; well, as unobtrusively as he could, with his height and build, down the side of the audience. He suddenly walked on to a roar of recognition from the audience. Eric looked at him. His face was saying, 'This is all we need, when we're just about to do a show.'

'Hello, Tom, what are you doing here?' Eric asked.

'I just thought I'd pop in and wish you luck,' Tom replied.

'Thank you. Ladies and gentlemen, Tommy Cooper!' said Eric.

Tom didn't move. Eric gave him an affectionate, but definite, push. Tom leant on him. If Tom leant on you, you stayed leant on. He was immovable. Eric looked desperate. Tom started to cry, which was something he could do to order.

'What's the matter, Tom?' asked Eric. (At the time, comedian Dick Emery was involved in much matrimonial chaos, having left his wife, gone back to her and left her again.) Tom wept copiously. Eric had given up. But he rallied and repeated the question, 'What's the matter, Tom?'

'Dick Emery's left me,' Tom cried, sobbing, as he stumbled off.

Tom and I were stranded at Manchester Airport, having been diverted due to fog. We went to the b*r. 'What are you having, Tommy?' The inquirer was a small man, who was obviously thrilled to meet Tommy.

'That's very kind of you,' Tom said.

'What are you doing here, Tommy?' asked the small man. (People always seemed to be asking him that.)

'Just walking about,' Tom replied.

'Pardon?' asked the man.

'Just walking about,' said Tom again.

The man smiled, uncomprehendingly and said, 'Oh.'

'I like walking about. I live in Chiswick, in London, and I walk about there a lot,' explained Tom.

The man now seemed anxious to escape.

'But I got fed up of walking around Chiswick, so Barry and I have come here, to do some walking about.'

All right, you had to be there, just for the pauses and the seriousness of the delivery. Nobody else could or would want to embark on a conversation like that. But he did. Just like that.

TWENTY-EIGHT

GET OFF! SORRY, I DON'T
DO REQUESTS

I'VE TOUCHED ON the subject of heckling already, although, as I said, it doesn't often happen in the after-dinner world. But, on the current comedy scene, it's practically a blood sport. At Malcolm Hardee's infamous Tunnel Club, you were lucky if the audience let you live.

Jeremy Hardy, who has appeared with us on *I'm Sorry, I Haven't a Clue*, did a classic put-down, after being heckled persistently by somebody in the audience. He stopped, looked and said, 'Simon, it's *over*.'

Mick Miller, a very funny comedian from the Blackpool area, was also being constantly interrupted one night. Finally, he said, 'This is unfair to that gentleman. I've got the microphone and the spotlight. He's in the dark. Put the spotlight on him.' The operator duly swung the light on to the man in question. 'No,' said Mick, 'that's just the beam; put the f* * * * *g thing on him.'

Johnny Hammond, a fine club comedian, was once performing in a boxing ring, in the good name of charity. It's theatre in the round and very difficult, as I know to my cost, having tried to entertain an audience on four sides at once. Johnny battled on and then Terry Downes, the boxer, climbed through the ropes and joined him. 'You've been too long in this ring,' he said to Johnny.

'Longer than you ever were,' said John.

Jo Brand told me that she went to see a comic working and he was having an especially tough time, with very little reaction. During one of many *longueurs*, a voice at the back said, '*Match of the Day*'s on.' Simple, but crushing.

Mike Hailey, whom I worked with on *The Stand-up Show*, tells the story of performing his *Star Trek* routine, in which he played all the characters. It always went well, but one night, in the mysterious way that sometimes happens, laughs were few and far between. He says himself that he actually ground to a halt. A voice in the dark said, 'This is comedy, Jim, but not as we know it.'

The amazing Lancashire comedian, Frank Randle, figures in a story that is not strictly about heckling, but demonstrates defiance under fire. Something of a legend in the North, he rarely appeared in London, where audiences had problems with his fruity patois. (I think I ordered that in a restaurant once.)

He journeyed South and appeared at London's Finsbury Park Empire. He met not with indifference, but outright hostility. Boos, catcalls and coins were thrown. The stage manager inflicted the supreme indignity on him by lowering the fire curtain, thereby terminating his act. Randle ducked beneath it and emerged, still face to face with his audience. 'Bastards!' he shouted.

He was summoned to the presence of Cissie Williams, a formidable woman, who booked the acts for the Moss Empire circuit. He arrived at her office, immaculately dressed and with his teeth in place. His appearance offstage was in dramatic contrast to his earthy theatrical persona. He was rebuked by Ms Williams, who said that language of that nature was not tolerated by his employers. Frank affected bewilderment.

'You called them bastards,' said Cissi.

'No, no,' protested Frank, 'have you the Italian?'

She was puzzled, as well she might be.

'I was shouting "Basta, basta!" – enough, enough!'

Ted Ray told me that he and friends were in the habit of attending matinées at the Palladium, where they gained free entry upon production of their union card. One day, they were intrigued to see on the programme an act billed as 'Harry Silverman – friend of the stars'. Halfway through the first half, the orchestra played an overture. An unusual thing happened at that stage of the proceedings. The curtains parted to reveal huge, blow-up pictures of film stars of the day: Gary Cooper, Marlene Dietrich, James Stewart, etc. In each photograph, there was a small man standing next to the star, beaming and creating the impression that he was a close and personal friend.

As the overture reached the climax, the same man burst through the central picture, which was made of paper. He then proceeded to do impressions of all the stars in the pictures, male and female. Ted later discovered that the man was a friend of a studio photographer and would hail the stars in the corridor or restaurant and rush up to them, while his friend would take the picture.

His act was abysmal. The audience was reduced to guessing who he was imitating and a rumble of discontent broke out. As with Frank Randle, the curtain was dropped on him. And, like Randle, he ducked under it to face the audience. Unlike Randle, he beamed at them and raised his arms, with a triumphant cry of 'Defeated!' The next day he was paid off and took the boat back to America.

Talking of fire curtains, which I was, they were definite features in theatres during that period, but are rarely seen now. They were heavy and were intended to seal off and prevent the spread of fire. And, occasionally, as I have indicated, to bring an end to any act the management disapproved of.

A double act were appearing at a provincial theatre. At the first performance on the Monday, they did their usual act. After the show, the manager came into their dressing room. 'It won't do,' he said, 'your act is too blue. This is a family theatre, so clean it up or you're out. If you do it again at this performance, I'll drop the fire curtain on you.'

He left. For the next hour, the two comics desperately tried to remember every clean joke they knew, to reconstruct their act. They went on at the second house and launched into their all-new, whiter-than-white act. It died. They ploughed on, but the laughs weren't coming. Suddenly, the comic said to his straight man, 'What's the difference between your wife and a submarine?'

Startled, his partner said, 'I don't know. What is the difference between my wife and a submarine?'

'I have never been inside a submarine,' said the comic. 'Mind your f* * * * *g head!'

Which all goes to show that it can be tough out there. As someone once said, 'When Pavarotti starts to sing "Nessum Dorma", nobody shouts, "Heard it!"'

PLEASE ACCEPT THIS AS AN INVOICE

From Colin Sell, Pianist on *I'm Sorry, I Haven't a Clue*

IF YOU WANT to know what Barry Cryer's like, catch his one-man show. As his pianist and friend, in my experience he is that affable man you see up there. He delights in the discovery and the telling of jokes, but, while he's ever ready to share his vast treasure trove of fun-bites, he recounts jokes neither to compare nor to impress. Just for the enjoyment of it. Nor, offstage and off-mike, does he feel the compulsion to be gag cracking all the time, as if permanently performing. He is that rarity: a generous human being first and a comedian second.

(Baz, is this OK? I'll take cash rather than a cheque, if you don't mind.)

TWENTY-NINE

CONSIDERED TRIFLES

MICHAEL PALIN, AT Graham Chapman's memorial service, held in the Great Hall of St Bartholomew Hospital, where Graham had been a student, told stories of Graham being late. He did actually seem to be in a different timescale to the rest of us. 'But I think, in a very real sense, he's here with us today,' said Michael. 'Well, he will be, in about twenty minutes.'

Roy Castle told me that, on the programme *Record Breakers*, they were filming an attempt to break the record for the world's largest musical chair competition. Scores of chairs, scores of contestants, bands and a huge crowd. Fun waxed fast and furious. Roy said he'd never forget the climactic moment. One man, circling two chairs.

Comedy in itself, comparatively harmless, can, however, have saddening side effects. One of our characters in the Kenny Everett show was an American general, Marvin D Bomb the Bastards.

He was a demented hawk in a jeep, with the stars and stripes fluttering on his helmet and guns firing from his epaulettes. His invariable solution to every problem was a cry of 'Bomb the bastards!'

During the Falklands War, my local pub was invaded by a crowd of exhilarated youths wearing T-shirts bearing that very legend. I toasted them, not too loudly: 'Here's to missing the point.'

After that war, a crippled man sat begging in a London street, with a card in front of him that read: 'VETERAN OF THE FALKLANDS WAR'. A passer-by dropped money in his hat.

'Graçias, señor,' said the man.

I sit here in an office overlooking the Regents Canal in London, watching the narrowboats pass the window and negotiate the two locks that are visible from here. This reminds me of the story of the out-of-work actor in Stratford-on-Avon, who got an audition in London. He had no money and decided he would have to hitch his way to the capital. One night, in a pub, he met the owner of a narrowboat that was going to London with a load of manure. He offered the actor a lift. He made himself a bed below deck and settled in. He was woken each time they arrived at a lock by the lock-keeper's cry of 'State your cargo!', to which the boatman would reply, 'Two tons of shit and an actor!'

After four locks, the actor went aloft. He spoke to the owner. 'Could I have a word with you about the billing?' he said.

Henry McGee told me he was talking to an old actor who showed him his scrapbook. They came upon a picture of the actor, young and handsome, gazing at Yorick's skull. 'Ah, you played Hamlet,' said Henry.

'No,' said the old thespian, 'Laertes; I borrowed the skull.'

I can hear Alan Bennett's vicar saying, 'And you know, I think that at some time in our lives we've all borrowed the skull.'

I was talking to David Renwick, old friend and author of *One Foot in the Grave*, about rehearsals for TV shows. David said that if the writer ever interjected with a comment about a particular bit of the action everyone would react as if to say, 'What's it got to do with you?' If the writer were to suggest, for instance, that an actor should pick up a teapot a moment earlier, this was regarded as an unwarranted intrusion. I told this to Keith Waterhouse, who thought the writer should say, 'I *am* the teapot!'

This book is dedicated to all my fellow teapots.

THIRTY

THIS IS YOUR DESERT ISLAND

I'VE BEEN LUCKY in achieving some of my ambitions. Everyone, I think, would like to appear on *Desert Island Discs*. I was invited by Michael Parkinson, or Sue Lawley as he's now known, some years ago. I remember that Herbert Morrison, the foreign secretary in the postwar Labour government, used to carry his choice of eight records with him at all times, just in case he was asked on the programme. Incidentally, Peter Mandelson is a descendant of Morrison. I treasure the thought of the arch spin doctor, watching the records revolve.

But I digress – which can go straight to your hips. Parky, the man who invented the revolutionary concept of a chat-show host who actually listens to his guests, and I were in the b*r at the BBC Television Centre. (I'm very well known at the centre, but not too well known round the edges.) Over a drink or two, he asked me on the programme. I accepted with alacrity and went home to think of eight favourite discs, with concomitant memories.

Noël Coward remarked how potent cheap music can be

and I resisted the temptation to choose eight worthy classics, in a pathetic attempt to convince people of my depth. Instead, I assembled seven jolly rock and roll and soul epics, plus 'Mars, the Bringer of War' from Holst's *Planet Suite*. I know, I know, we're back on planet cliché, but I love it. It was the signature tune of *The War of the Worlds* on the radio when I was a kid, and it has lodged in my subconscious ever since.

I referred earlier to the evocative power of smells, and music is the aural equivalent. The moment I hear 'Unchained Melody' – Al Hibbler, *not* Jimmy Young – I'm back at Leeds University and in love. Aural sex indeed. Come to think of it, I remember when Jimmy Young *was*.

Subsequently, my wife and I were invited to a *Desert Island Discs* anniversary party at the Reform Club. It was amazing. Every surviving prime minister – and Edward Heath – was there, and so many other notable people; it was like a living Madame Tussaud's, except marginally more lifelike. The ailing Jeremy Thorpe made a rare appearance and Bamber Gascoigne, or Jeremy Paxman as he's now known, and I compared notes.

My favourite memory of the programme was the appearance of Gary Glitter, who chose as his luxury item an inflatable woman and a tin of Elastoplast. When informed that he could only have one, he immediately replied, 'A tin of Elastoplast.'

Elizabeth Schwarzkopf, the singer, chose eight of her own

records. But then again, her name in English is Betty Blackhead. I can assure you that my number one in Finland did not figure in my selection.

There was such a reaction to Kenny Everett's appearance on the programme, when he talked of being HIV positive and his early life, that people who said they'd never liked him told me that they'd revised their opinion.

I was told the story of Roy Plomley, the creator of the show and its original host, who took guests to the Garrick Club prior to the recording. He made the choice of guests himself and had, on this occasion, selected Alistair McLean, the novelist. McLean, a somewhat reclusive man, was rarely photographed, and Roy was obviously intrigued. They had lunch and chatted of this and that, but nothing relevant to his writing. When they started the programme, one of Roy's early questions was: 'How many books have you written?' This was met with some bafflement by his guest, who replied that he'd only written one: something on the lines of *Where to Eat in Deal*. Confusion reigned. Light dawned. They'd got the wrong Alistair McLean. This man was from the Tourist Authority. But they did the programme anyway. I believe they had a similar experience with Martin Bormann, a plumber from Esher.

Not everyone wants to be caught by *This Is Your Life*. Danny Blanchflower, the footballer, walked away when greeted by Eamonn Andrews. Richard Gordon, the author of *Doctor in the House* books, uttered an expletive, but was persuaded to stay. Tommy Cooper, on the programme for the actor Bill Fraser, behaved as if the victim was Joe Frazier, the boxer. Much mirth ensued.

I appeared on it some seven or eight times, in a friend and colleague capacity, but I realised that I was beginning to look like rent-a-guest. When Bernard Cribbins was targeted, my wife and I were invited to be in the audience, but not on the programme. Afterward, Eamonn told me that, when my name was mentioned at a meeting as a possible participant, it got a laugh and I was barred from then on.

The phone rang; it was Willie Rushton. (He used to do an impression of a phone.) 'They want us to do a programme about double acts with old Tooky,' he said. I knew he was referring to my doppelgänger, Barry Took. Nearly every day of my life, I am taken for the other Barry, on one occasion by Princess Anne – but that's a story involving heads of state and an international conspiracy that must wait for another time.

'That's fine,' I said.

'Do you really think so?' said Willie. He was playing his usual game of going against the tide.

'Yes, why not?' I said.

'Ah well, I'll do it, if you do,' he said.

I realised later that this was all an act: he knew that if he seemed too enthusiastic I would have been suspicious. I also realised that if I had agreed with him and said no the programme would have to be rethought or scrapped.

On the Sunday in question, we turned up at Teddington Studios to meet Barry. All that afternoon, my wife had been saying, 'You're not wearing those trousers, are you?' As I was, it was a baffling question. We went into the studio. There was a simple, not to say awful, set. Willie and I sat on a settee. Barry began to introduce the show to the audience. He was reading from cards and I remember thinking it was all very offhand. But, then again, it was only a pilot for a proposed series. Suddenly, I became aware that someone had joined us. I thought at first it was the floor manager, but it was Michael Aspel with the red book. My second thought was that Willie was the victim, but then I recalled that they had already done him and I had been on it. My third thought was apparently confirmed – it was going to be Tooky.

Michael said, 'Barry...' He paused and then said my name.

It's a strange out-of-body experience – totally unreal.

Jokes about my trousers proliferated; family and friends came on; Brenda from Leeds University all those years ago, now a postmistress in Suffolk, came back into my life and, glory of glories, I notice a piano with a trumpet on top. Piano? Trumpet? On came Colin Sell, the definitive pianist, and then Humphrey Lyttelton. Colin announced that I was going to sing 'Show Me the Way to Go Home' accompanied by himself and Humph. My cup runneth over. I would sing with Humph before shuffling off this mortal coil.

What other ambitions achieved? I have appeared on the *Sooty Show*, so there doesn't seem anything left; apart, that is, from my lifelong dream of eating a prawn sandwich without some of the prawns falling out.

Regrets. I've had a few, but, then again, too few to mention.

THIRTY-ONE

FIRST ACT

IN EARLY 1998 I performed in my first play. No one seems to believe this, but it's true. Over forty years of performing in various modes, not to say media (so I won't), but never a play.

I had, in fact, acted once before in *Emergency Ward 10* in the sixties. (Note for younger reader: This was a pioneer hospital series on ITV, the *ER* of its day.)

I played a bad comedian, involved in some mystery, the details of which are now mysterious to me. Why I was cast as a bad comedian is still a source of some misgiving; why did they think of me? Draw your own conclusions and colour them in later.

In the cast were actors Pauline Jameson, with whom I still exchange Christmas cards; John Wood, and John Carlisle, a pillar of the RSC. I met him on *Call My Bluff* after over thirty years.

One of the nicest things about reaching my age is the number of people who appear out of the woodwork, after being out of your life for many years. I was once visited in my dressing room by a man with whom I had worked at Leeds Highways Department in 1955. He immediately embarked on a rundown of what had happened to all our colleagues since then. I even remembered some of the names. Some, of course, were dead.

When you are young, you are immortal. Anyone over thirty is old. Then you get to the age when people your age die. This gives pause for thought. When people younger than you shuffle off this mortal coil, I must confess to a momentary reaction of 'I've got seven years on you', as if you're winning some grim race. Not praiseworthy, but there we are. Where are we, incidentally? Ah yes, the play.

But, before I get to that, one more incident concerning the passing of the years. I never joined my school's old boys' association. In fact, I never kept in touch in any way, as I left Leeds in 1957. Nearly thirty years later, I was tracked down by them and asked to speak at a dinner in London. I went along expecting to meet one or two contemporaries, which indeed I did, but what astonished me was that two masters I remembered were there.

I was stunned. One was 78 and the other 82. I realised that when I was at school they would have been in their forties. *Old*. One of them even claimed to remember me, but I think that was kindness. Or maybe not. In their dedicated lives, they seemed to acquire a fantastic memory for names. Mr Chips with everything.

David Frost has this gift. He remembered my mother

after a gap of over five years, reminisced about the fourth-floor flat in Maida Vale with no lift, and then produced two bottles of champagne as he'd found out it was my birthday. Or had he remembered?

I was standing at the counter of the London Weekend Television canteen with Arthur Askey when a large man approached, punched Arthur on the arm and beamed, 'You don't remember me, do you?'

Arthur looked up at him. 'Isle of Wight, 1938,' he said. 'You were the stage manager and you were bloody useless.'

Meanwhile, back at the Leeds Grammar School dinner. On the back of the menu was the school song, in Latin. At one point in the evening, we rose to sing it. I sang it all the way through, without looking at the words. They had been lurking in my head for all those years. Have I mentioned memory in this book before? I can't remember. My theory is that the brain never discards information, but pushes it to the back, where it lies doggo, waiting to be called on.

My memory for jokes is notorious; my recall of more important matters not so. Johnny Speight claimed that he once forgot his wife's name and asked one of the children, 'You – tall one with the glasses – what's your mother's name?' True story; as true as I'm riding this camel.

Eddie Judd, the actor, told me that he once met a former amour in the canteen at the BBC. Would her name come back to him? No. 'Darling!' he cried and they fell into conversation. She mentioned she was playing a nurse in the play

194 • *Barry Cryer*

she was recording and then went to get two more cups of tea. Eddie looked at the script she had left on the table. The actress playing the nurse was called Barbara. Of course, Barbara! When she returned, he Barbara'd her to death. They travelled back to their respective rehearsals in the lift and it arrived at her floor.

As she stepped out, she said to Eddie, 'There are two nurses in this play, Eddie, but nice try.'

I've mentioned Korsakoff syndrome before in this narrative, haven't I? It can involve short-term memory loss. Bill Cosby has his own theory on this. He cites the common experience of going upstairs and then forgetting why he did so. He believes your memory leaves your head and moves to your arse, because you come downstairs, sit down and immediately spring up, exclaiming, 'I've remembered!'

Pardon? Oh yes, the play. I have done four pantomimes in my life, in three of which I've played the dame. More of that later. The point I'm making now is that I've never been so tired in my life as when pantoing. Two shows a day, every day, even when children have gone back to school. Some friends of mine have done three. As time goes on, the matinées are either deserted or populated by senior citizens, who are most welcome but hardly disposed to leap up on stage, join in community singing and leave with a bag of sweets. So, when I was offered a role on an Ayckbourn play in 1997, to run through Christmas and the new year, I accepted with alacrity. I've always believed in frightening myself, as my mirror will testify, and the thought of actually learning lines and being faithful to the text galvanised me into action. If you forget your lines in the pantomime or the other stage shows I do, you refer to the fact, mess around, change tack and wander down another avenue. But my respect for writers is firmly ingrained, particularly when they are of Ayckbourn's calibre.

A friend of years ago, introduced to me by Bernard Cribbins, was Alf Bradley, a veteran BBC radio producer and much respected guru. He once remarked to me that a young producer who had worked for him 'writes a bit, and he's good'. A pithy definition of Alan Ayckbourn.

The first play of his I ever saw was *Relatively Speaking*, which featured a garden. Then there was the trilogy *The Norman Conquests*, which featured, on different nights, a house *and* a garden. *Bedroom Farce* – a house again. What was this man, playwright or architect? His incredibly interlocking plots, with the action taking place at different times, fascinated me, and I tried to see every successive production. I soon realised that he wasn't just about tricks, but pain. Everyone he writes about is, in some way, a loser. His characters lead, in the classic phrase, 'lives of quiet desperation', which are sometimes not so quiet. Their eruptions, when they reach snapping point, are some of the most impressive in British theatre.

In the summer of 1997, Ian Liston, a friend of some years (duration of friendship, not age), for whom I would appear in music-hall shows, sent me *Season's Greetings*, Ayckbourn's play about a Christmas from hell, experienced by a family and friends. The part Ian wanted me to play was Uncle Harvey, who can best be described as a psychopathic couch potato. He spends the entire first scene watching television, with his back to the action. Thus, as you sit there, the story starts to unfold as if it were a radio play. Initially, I had no idea who was where and who had just come on or gone off. In fact, one night, when one of the actors missed his entrance and didn't appear, I was only aware of a silence, followed by unintelligible noise from one of the others. I barged in with my next line and we proceeded.

But back to the beginning. After reading the play, I said yes and the die was cast. I was cast to die. I arrived at the Drill Hall, off Tottenham Court Road, on the first day of rehearsals. The reception from the other members of the cast was cordial. I relaxed, but I wondered if there was a lingering suspicion about this aging jokesmith who was presuming to join their ranks. They told me later that this was not so, but at the time my paranoia was intact. Although easily the oldest member of the cast, I was the novice. A worrying combination.

After the usual desultory chat and introductions, we sat round a table to read the script. I was aware, even then, that Oliver, the youngest, appeared to know all his lines already and, apparently, everybody else's. This unnerved me. I rendered Uncle Harvey in my native Leeds tones – why shouldn't an uncle be a Yorkshireman, I reasoned? This met with the director's approval; or was he just leaving me alone for a while?

Rehearsals progressed and the 'blocking' began, i.e. the moves round the floor, with tape representing walls and doors thereon.

*Digression. There was an actor called Wilfred Lawson whose ability not only to act brilliantly but in the process steal the show while under the influence was much admired. How can I put this? He and the grape were not strangers. One day he was rehearsing a television play, with the afore-mentioned tape on the floor. As the action of the play proceeded, Wilfred persisted in walking through a wall. A door is represented on the floor by an angled piece of tape, suggesting the door is ajar. But Wilfred cheerfully ignored this and continually stepped over the tape that served as the wall. Finally, the director stopped him and insisted that he observe the door. The next time Wilfred made to go through the 'door', he made an elaborate piece of mime, opening the door, closing it, and then, taking a piece of paper from his pocket, he scribbled on it and mimed sliding it under the door. Exasperated, the director asked him what he was doing now. 'Handing in my fucking resignation,' said Wilfred.

I met Wilfred once in the Cottage Club, off Charing Cross Road. A small figure, in a full-length coat, nursing a large bubble glass of brandy. I was introduced and told him how much I enjoyed his work.

'How kind,' he said. 'A quadruple brandy would suffice.'

I laughed politely, but he meant it and gravely toasted me; he downed it in one.

He appeared at the Royal Court Theatre in *Kelly's Eye* with Nicol Williamson. Wilfred had disappeared on one of his usual perambulations during rehearsals and was nowhere to be seen. Nicol exploded and, standing in the stalls, delivered a blistering tirade on the subject of this unreliable, unemployable, drunk. He paused for breath. From the darkness at the back of the theatre came Wilfred's voice as he said, 'I thought that speech had been cut.'

One of his last appearances was in *The Likely Lads* with James Bolam and Rodney Bewes. In an almost incomprehensible scene with them in the pub, Wilfred walked off with the whole thing.

What does this prove? Many fine actors do not need alcohol to fuel their muse. Many have needed it and still do. Robert Newton would be made up at film studios, still wearing the pyjamas and dressing gown in which he had been picked up that morning. After a deep breath, he would do a flawless take. Some artists' spirits have been licensed. Let's leave it at that.

Back to the play. Rehearsals continued. On the second day, I had my panic attack. I had taken the play home (Arthur Lowe once said he wouldn't have a script in the house) and I reread the whole thing. After marking my character's lines in yellow, I realised there were a lot of them. I'll never learn all this, my febrile brain kept repeating, and my ever patient wife had to endure an impassioned speech of how I would go in the next day and ask to be released. Hard to believe now, but it happened.

I duly asked for a chat with Kit, the director, and producer Ian. They smilingly ignored my request and I went back to work.

A strange process takes place in the learning of lines. Apart from Oliver, the memory man, most actors – using the word in the unisex sense – seem to absorb the lines in conjunction with the moves the director gives them. If you're going through a door, you tend to remember the lines you say as you do so. My friend Robert Powell – the man who played Christ and won – told me he was rehearsing a play called *Tovarich* at Chichester. (The play was not called 'Tovarich at Chichester', which conjures up a totally different picture.) He was appearing with Natalia Makarova, the former ballerina *assoluta*, who now performs as an actress and singer. (So many of us 'greats' have changed track later in our careers.) At the dress rehearsals, he suddenly realised that Makarova wasn't standing where she should be, but behind him. He stopped and asked what she was doing.

'I'm a free spirit, darling; I go where I please,' she replied.

'All right,' said Bob, 'what's your next line?'

She couldn't remember. But once she went back to her original position, the line returned.

This principle dawned on me as we rehearsed. The more I moved, the more the lines started to lodge in my brain.

During rehearsals, Chris, one of the cast who soon became a drinking companion, and I were in the Rising Sun pub in Tottenham Court Road. Alun Armstrong, who was rehearsing *The Front Page* and was in the area, entered, greeted us and came over. I asked him how it was going. 'The lines won't go in,' he said, 'it's getting harder as I get older.' I clinked his glass. If a vastly experienced thespian like Alun experiences the sensation, I thought, maybe I'm in good company. Needless to say, the play opened and he got rave reviews. This memory thing was further emphasised when my wife and I went to see David Hare's play *Amy's View* at the National Theatre. Talking to Judi Dench afterward (are you keeping score of the name-drops? I'm not), she confided that she, too, had had a panic attack during rehearsals and tried to leave. The sequel was that, like Alun, she has had an enormous success in the play. I was beginning to think that it affected only the best people. But that wore off.

Halfway through rehearsals, I took part in a memorial show for Willie Rushton, which I'd been asked to put together. I've never been involved in any show where I asked people to appear and everybody said yes immediately. Humphrey Lyttelton and his band, Peter O'Toole, Tim Rice, Auberon Waugh, Graeme Garden and Colin Sell from Clue, all the singers who'd appeared in *Two Old Farts in the Night*, the aforementioned Robert Powell . . . On and on it went. The night was joyful, culminating in an all-star kazoo band, accompanying a tape of Willie singing 'Neasden', which he wrote for one of those plastic records that used to be attached to the cover of *Private Eye*. Remember those? I like the word 'celebrate' in terms of remembering those who have gone, and that night was certainly a celebration.

The morning after, I journeyed to Farnham, where rehearsals continued. By the opening night, though the words were in place, with a little help from a copy of the *Radio Times* with cue lines in the inside page, my bottle certainly wasn't, in place that is. For the benefit of those not acquainted with the word 'bottle' in this context, let me explain.

One of the most common manifestations of nerves is the tweaking of the buttocks – a positive response in the sphincter area. 'Bottle' is short for 'bottle and glass', which rhymes with 'arse'. Get the picture? My bottle, therefore, was poised to launch the play.

The opening night came and went in a daze of 'getting through it'. This is not to suggest that anyone gives less than their best, but the audience is regaled with the sight of people on the stage operating on automatic pilot; you can practically *see* the adrenaline. From then on, the routine sets in.

Touring is a world apart; you are gypsies on the road. It is a world I knew well, but in recent years I've got into the habit of staying in hotels. I was lucky to be able to do so, but I got accustomed to it and never gave it a thought. I soon realised that my colleagues in the play didn't have the where-withal to lead this lifestyle and were industriously consulting digs lists in search of lodgings in each of the towns we visited. I joined in, not wishing to appear a 'lardi' (short for 'la de da', or w****r). I was extremely glad that I did, otherwise I would have been distanced from the gang in a sort of artistic apartheid. Nights of fish and chips, finger-lickin'-good, bacon sarnies, quizzes until the early hours in a cottage outside Bury St Edmunds. Somebody said to me, patronisingly, that I was being rather patronising, but I assured them that it was pure selfish pleasure. But, then again, whoever admitted to being patronising?

* Digression. Someone once accused Stephen Fry of patronising them, upon which he put his arm around them and, smiling patiently, said, 'No, no. Let me tell you what patronising *really* means.'

It was also Stephen who met a man who said, 'I wish I had a tenth of your talent.'

Stephen replied, 'Your wish has been granted.'

Talking of p*********g, one thing that has always annoyed me is the implicit snobbery of some critics who seem to regard comedy as some lower form of life. Prunella Scales appeared in a play at the Old Vic and a scribe wrote: 'She proved that she was more than just a sitcom actress.' She had just been doing *Fawlty Towers* with John Cleese, for God's sake. Wasn't that acting of the highest calibre?

Jimmy Jewel, Dave King, Roy Hudd and the afore-mentioned Max Wall were all comedians who went on to distinguished acting careers. Beryl Reid was a stand-up comic before triumphing in *The Killing of Sister George* and many other roles, including her portrayal of Queenie in *Smiley's People*.

The art of stand-up, as it is now graphically known, is the most concentrated, gruelling and demanding branch of our profession. There, I've said it.

Donald Sinden, a man who has played Lear and appeared in Ray Cooney farces, said that he was in no doubt which was harder. And he didn't mean Lear. In America, Jackie Gleason and Alan King went from comedy success to acting in films. In his film of *Henry V*, Laurence Olivier cast come-dian George Robey as Falstaff, transplanting the character from *Henry IV*, and, more recently, Kenneth Branagh chose Ken Dodd to play (a mute), Yorick, in *Hamlet*. A mute Doddy is a thought to conjure with. Branagh used the full, uncut version of *Hamlet* for his film – how appropriate for Ken, whose marathon stage performances are legendary.

I mentioned earlier that I had rarely been accused of acting, but I was forgetting my ground-breaking portrayal of Robert Maxwell. You never heard of that? I'm not surprised. The story goes as follows . . .

I met an amazing character called Evan Steadman, who had worked with Captain Bob and had, in fact, sold his company to him for sixteen million pounds. And he got the money. Whose money is open to conjecture, but he got it. Evan was recording an album of songs, celebrating, if that's the word, the notorious Maxwell. The music was by Sir Arthur Sullivan; the lyrics were new. Evan saw me in an old Broadway musical at the Barbican and thought I was right for the part. When I pointed out that I had white hair and glasses and, while not exactly sylphlike, my figure was hardly of Maxwellian proportions, he agreed that that was irrelevant to the record, but offered me the stage role. I was bewildered.

Rehearsals commenced some weeks later in a Welsh club in Gray's Inn Road in London. I joined a cast of seasoned professionals feeling very apprehensive indeed. A foretaste of the Ayckbourn play, now I come to think of it. The music had already been programmed into a computer, which meant the keys of the song and the tempo were already predetermined. This was a unique situation, leaving no room for manoeuvre. It discarded that quaint old notion of working with a human being at a piano who adapts the songs according to yourlimitations. As if this wasn't worrying enough, with fast patter songs to cope with, I was still aghast at the thought of looking even remotely like him. I needn't have worried. I met a brilliant make-up artist, Pat Hay, who had a black wig made for me and proceeded to pluck my eyebrows. She had studied Maxwell videos and photographs and noticed that he had abbreviated eyebrows. I observed his characteristic slit-eyed expression and the picture began to fall into place. A fat suit was produced and Pat gave my face the florid, broken-veined look of the arch rogue. I must point out that my appearance was to be for one night only initially, in front of an audience of prospect brokers, ticket agencies, etc. From then on – who knew?

Came the night. The venue was Imagination, off Tottenham Court Road, a vast glass and steel edifice, like something out of *Blade Runner*. The cast twitched and the computer hummed. My role seemed to consist mainly of trying to keep up with the infernal machine and barking, 'You're fired!' at regular intervals.

The show went well, but I still had misgivings. To portray Maxwell as some sort of jolly buccaneer seemed to be totally wrong. A bleaker approach, more akin to Sondheim, would have been nearer the mark. In addition, despite mention of further rehearsals and new songs, nobody seemed to mention money. Call me nit-picking, but this is my living and if remuneration isn't mentioned I tend to lose interest. So, after my brief burst of glory, if that's the word I'm looking for, I left the production. Evan and I remained on the best of terms; indeed, my wife and I visited him and his family in the south of France, where he lives in what you can in no way describe as penury.

The role of Maxwell was subsequently played, also for just one night, by Desmond Barritt of the Royal Shakespeare Company, and finally landed in the lap of John Savident, currently to be seen as the egregious Fred in *Coronation*

Street. But it was not to be. Four days before the opening night, the show was injuncted and never opened. The Maxwell lawyers had objected to the depiction of the sons, Ian and Kevin, and Betty, the great widow. I seriously think the show could have been picketed, quite understandably, by outraged *Mirror* pensioners and may well have turned out to be a hugely unpopular, not to mention unprofitable, venture. [That's enough about Maxwell. You're fired, Ed.]

Back to the play, which I mentioned some several pages ago. It was an education. As I said, I realised I had been cosseted on tour for some years, staying in hotels. The average actor can't afford this, so I joined the others in digs. Buying rounds in the pubs has to be carefully monitored before it gets out of hand. Thursday night is eagerly awaited – pay night. Clive, another good new friend, was delighted to obtain a job which would commence the week after the play closed. This necessitated him rehearsing in London every day, then dashing to King's Cross to catch the train to Peterborough. At night, he would dash off to catch a train back, finally arriving home in Manor Park some time after 1.00 a.m., then up again the next morning to rehearse. I watched him visibly tiring as the week progressed. I suggested that he would be better off getting a good night's sleep in Peterborough and catching an early train to London in the morning. He looked at me and said, 'Digs and transport, Baz?' The point was taken.

Our safari took us from Farnham in Surrey to Cheltenham, Bury St Edmunds and thence to Peterborough.

Each theatre and its town, of course, has its own character. The Redgrave Theatre in Farnham, for instance, is in the middle of a moneyed catchment area, but is surrounded by other theatres in Guildford, Basingstoke, Aldershot, et al. (The theatre in 'al' is, admittedly, quite small.) Therefore, at Christmas, Farnham decided to present a play instead of a pantomime for the benefit of those without younger children to entertain. Thus they chose the Ayckbourn play, which is about Christmas, albeit the darker side of Yule, subscribing to the theory that Christmas is when we meet the people we've been avoiding all year.

Next on the itinerary was the Everyman Theatre, Cheltenham, an old stamping ground of mine. I worked there with Willie Rushton and also in music hall, cavorting in a kilt and tam-o'-shanter, risking prosecution under the Trade Description Act, considering my place of birth. Now here was a total change of pace and ambience.

One evening, I was in the b*r, embarking on my preshow pint, when I found myself standing next to a man who was studying the brochure that detailed the delights to come at the theatre in the next month. He was gazing at the photograph of me.

'Where do I know him from?' he asked Matt, the barman.

Matt looked at me and then back at the man. 'Oh, he has been around for ever,' said Matt.

'*Points of View* on the telly,' affirmed the man.

Now it was my turn. 'No, that was Barry Took,' I said.

I have to say, in fairness, that I was sporting a brutal haircut, reminiscent of Magwitch in *Great Expectations*, and was not wearing my glasses.

'You're right,' said the man. 'So where do I know him from?' he asked again.

'I thought he was dead anyway,' I twinkled.

'But I hear he is very good in this,' the man said.

Oh, come on, allow an old man his moment.

We chatted on for a few moments while Matt turned his back and snorted at the optics. I realised that this was getting silly and rather sadistic and, to be honest, pathetic vanity on my part, so I broke the news to my companion that I was the man in the picture. He actually blushed charmingly and apologised. I assured him there was no need and bought him a guilty pint. We talked on and he told me he was fascinated by 'you people'. Then he delivered the *coup de grâce*.

'Do you get paid for this?' he asked.

I assured him that I did.

'My sister is a sculptor,' he said, 'and she hasn't earnt a penny in ten years.'

We parted, with him assuring me that he would be in to see the play. He never did.

I've already referred to the bursting of the ego balloon, which is so essential for mental health. A friend of mine appeared at an arts festival in a small town and several of the locals threw open their houses as dressing rooms and lodgings. Four of the artists were in the front room of a cottage when there was a knock on the door. The owner entered, apologised and asked if he could take a photograph. They gladly agreed and, pulling up their trousers, posed in a group. He turned his back on them and took a picture of the room.

'Thank you,' he said, 'you see, I'm selling the place.'

Arthur Askey was in a lift and a fellow occupant said, 'You don't half look like Arthur Askey.'

Arthur confirmed that he was often told that.

Later in the week, he met the man again. 'Arthur's staying in the hotel,' he said.

'What a coincidence,' said Arthur, and broke the news that he was, in fact, the genuine article.

The man laughed and said, 'I bet you wish you were.'

As a writer, I was often in a position to see egos in public view. I stood next to a certain well-known comedian at reception at the BBC Television Centre. His Rolls-Royce, complete with chauffeur in matching livery, was parked directly outside and was visible through the window. A man at the desk spoke. 'Whose is that bloody ostentatious Rolls?' he inquired. The silence from the comedian was deafening, but I can still remember the twitching of the face muscles.

I once arrived at a party to be greeted by the host in ebullient mood, not to say pissed as a newt. 'This is Barry Cryer!' he announced to the throng, who appeared somewhat underwhelmed by this information. 'He is the best

joke teller I know! Tell them the one about the elephant!'
he continued.

Can you imagine a more effective way of turning a roomful
of strangers into potential enemies? No, neither can I. I hesi-
tatingly told the pachydermic anecdote, which was actually
quite funny, but obviously the omens were not good. It was
greeted with silence and then a return to general conversation and a certain turning of backs.

I slunk past two party-goers engaged in conversation and
I heard one say, 'Someone's ego has just fled screaming from
the room.'

The stiletto was now firmly in my ribs. Time passed . . .
I met people who apparently wished me no harm and then
I decided to leave. As I passed the man who made the
scathing comment, he said, 'Leaving?'

'Yes,' I said, 'my ego is outside on a meter.'

I don't want to imply that this was some kind of competition that I finally won, but merely quote the incident to
illustrate how a situation can suddenly run out of control
and it's not your fault!

BAZ AND HIS FILOFAGS

By Graeme Garden

WHAT CAN ONE say about Barry Cryer that has not been better said before about other people?

I first became aware of Barry (or Baz, as he affects to prefer) at the legendary round table of the Algonquin Hotel in Cardiff. He was the leading light of the gag-writing team assembled to provide topical material for Prince Yusupov, whose image was considered to be in need of a bit of a burnish following the unpleasant business with Rasputin. Barry's previous employer, Ramsay MacDonald, was said to be sorry to see him go, and, as anyone who witnessed 'Ramsay Mac's' last season at the Alhambra in Macclesfield can tell you, Barry's talents were sadly missed by that grand old stager.

I joined the team as a humble assistant, providing the 'Cryer clan', as they were known, with copius quantities of sweet tea and lager and clearing up after SJ Perelman.

In a very real sense, Barry Cryer took me under his wing. He would laugh merrily at any little quip I managed to come up with, and immediately jot it down on his packet of menthol cigarettes; his 'filofags' as he always called it, which was to become a hilarious topical joke many years later when the Filofax was invented. For me it was rewarding enough to see my little 'squibs' included in the final script. Indeed, it had to be rewarding enough, as nothing else was on offer.

Barry learnt his trade at the school of Hard Knocks (a wee village not far from Aberdeen) where a love of comedy was literally beaten in to him. There he followed a long apprenticeship in the service of Little Tich and, much later, Richard Todd.

The lessons he picked up in those early years were to stand him in good stead. To this very day, hardened old pros will recognise one of the maestro's bons mots as once again it swims to the surface of some TV comedy showcase, and they will turn to each other, smiling as they murmur the name of Barry Cryer.

THIRTY-TWO

AFTERTHOUGHTS

FINALLY, THE TRAIN of thought has reached the terminus, or maybe just a siding. Thank you for sharing the trip. What thoughts remain as I sit in my sheltered accommodation? The curtains are drawn, but the rest of the room is real. The fire crackles in the grate and Matron has brought me a mug of spiked Ribena. She tells me that she's taken the joint out of the oven. It's rather charred, but still smokeable. I was sitting in my library, musing over memories this afternoon, when the woman came and told me the library was closing. On the way home, I heard the sound of a piano coming from an upstairs window. Luckily, I managed to jump out of the way.

It's been over fifty years since I entered show business and I'm still looking for a way out. Nineteen hundred and fifty-seven – the year of Nasser in Egypt, Anthony Eden in Britain, and Gromyko in Russia; the Duke of Edinburgh embarked on a world tour; Archbishop Makarios returned from exile; petrol rationing ended; the first British hydrogen bomb was detonated near Christmas Island; the first Russian satellite, Sputnik 1, was launched; the Jodrell Bank telescope went into operation; the Queen made her first television Christmas broadcast. Dwarfing all these events was my arrival in London, on a seventeen-day return rail ticket.

I've celebrated friends no longer with us, but other names come to mind. Dennis Potter, who appeared in one of the most poignant TV programmes, talking about his impending death with Melvyn Bragg.

One day, after watching *The Singing Detective* the night before, I happened to hear Derek Jameson on the radio. It was an accident, I tell you! Referring to the show and the fearsome psoriasis with which Michael Gambon was covered, he opined, 'Who wants to see a bloke with cirrhosis?' I wrote to Dennis, informing him of Derek's malapropism.

He wrote back: 'As regards cirrhosis, I don't know about the actor, but the author's well on his way.'

The name-drops in this book constitute a flood, but there are still a few more I haven't lobbed like grenades into the narrative.

I only met John Gielgud once. It was in reception at the old LWT studios in Wembley. I was waiting for someone and noticed the unique profile standing nearby. In his mouth was the habitual Turkish cigarette and he was patting his pockets. I approached and proffered my lighter.

'Thank you,' he said, making it sound like a soliloquy.

I lit his cigarette.

'What do you do?' he asked.

'I'm a writer,' I replied.

'I'm an actor,' he said.

I once spoke to Marilyn Monroe. During one of my frequent periods of 'resting' – show-business euphemism for unemployment – I was working in the Paul Cave office in London. Paul, as I mentioned before, was Frankie Vaughan's manager and employed me, between occasional bouts of work, to deal with fan mail and general correspondence. Around this time, Frank had made a film with Marilyn and Yves Montand entitled *Let's Make Love*. A phone link-up had been set up between London and Los Angeles for a press conference. The phone rang and I picked it up. A voice at the other end said, 'I have Miss Monroe for you.'

A pause.

'Hello!' I gulped.

'Who is this?' asked the goddess.

I gave her my name, but refrained from my biography. I was mainly preoccupied with signalling to someone else to pick up the phone. We chatted, and she was charming. I handed over the phone. End of story, save merely to say that I spoke to Marilyn Monroe. I spoke to Marilyn Monroe.

Mel Brooks and his wife, Anne Bancroft, visited their friend, Dom De Luise, at Elstree Studios. I was introduced to him: 'Mel, this is Barry Cryer.'

'Never mind,' said Mel.

I worked with an American comedian called George Gobel, forgotten now, perhaps, a gentle, whimsical soul, with a formidable capacity for drink. We met at the Savoy Hotel and took tea, which was apparently one of his lifetime ambitions. He was immaculate in blazer and slacks and conversed in his usual quiet tones. He looked around at the members of the tea parties at other tables, all chatting inaudibly. He sighed contentedly. Then, 'Yahoo!!' he bellowed, an ear-splitting hog call. The effect was electric. I won't say that cups were dropped, but jaws were. The shock passed. George looked at me and smiled. 'One for the book,' he said. I've put it in mine, George.

When the night of the recording of our shows came, it became apparent that George was – how shall I put this? – somewhat worsened by wear. He stood in front of the camera and the audience and was swaying slightly. But it was visible. What to do?

'Go with him,' said the director to the cameraman.

The camera began to move imperceptibly, compensating for George's side-to-side movement. The cameraman was bought a large drink afterwards. George bought his own.

That night, he left for his hotel, stuffing ice cubes into his pockets, telling me, 'They might come in handy later.'

I was told he once appeared on *The Gary Moore Show* on American television. Moore was the nonsmoking, non-drinking, archetypal Mr Clean of the medium. Just before recording, George said to him, 'Fancy a little drink, Gary?'

'No, thank you, George,' replied the host, 'I never drink before a show.'

George looked at him in wonder. 'You mean you go on alone?' he asked.

I miss him.

One of my favourite people is an agent, Michael Black, brother of lyricist Don. Michael had an office in Great Windmill Street, off Piccadilly Circus, above a salt-beef bar. Their ceiling, i.e. his floor, was so thin that he could stamp his foot and they would hear it clearly. They evolved a code. One stamp meant a cup of tea, two indicated a cup of coffee, and three a salt-beef sandwich. 'It worked very well,' said Michael, 'until the day I auditioned a flamenco dancer in the office.'

He was once visited by a representative of the Board of Customs and Excise to discuss VAT. After sundry chat, Michael mooted that they should get down to business: how much was involved? The man mentioned a large sum of money.

'Do you take cash?' asked Michael.

Rather taken aback, the man said he didn't see why not. Michael opened a drawer and took out a large wad of notes. 'Would you like a receipt?' asked the man.

'A receipt for cash? Are you mad?' said Michael.

He told me he got a call one day asking for 'two Jacks' (rhyming slang: 'Jack the Ripper' – stripper). He was somewhat offended by this, having moved on in his career, well beyond the booking of such exotic artistes. The caller mentioned money and Michael suddenly remembered where he could acquire two Jacks. Now I can vouch for the fact that Michael takes a keen personal interest in his clients. He often appears at dinners where I am speaking, to check that all is well. So, on the night in question, he turned up to ensure the welfare of the Jack duet. He stood on the side of the stage, watching them discard their garments. There was a man standing next to him, who turned and said, 'Pop on and pick up their clothes.'

'I beg your pardon,' said Michael, 'do you know who I am?'

'No,' said the man, 'do you know who I am?'

'No,' said Michael.

'I'm the guy who's paying for this. Who are you?' asked the man.

'I'm the man who pops on and picks up their clothes,' said Michael.

Michael, the commission is in the post.

Someone else who I was inordinately fond of was the actor Bill Franklyn. He told me about a friend of his who was invited to a fancy-dress party. He decided not to bother with a costume, but as the day drew near he thought he owed it to his host. The theme was black and white. He hired a nun's costume. It was a hot night and he sat in the corner, sweating profusely and regretting the whole thing. An Australian came up and sat down next to him. 'I find your costume very tasteless,' he said.

'Well,' said Bill's friend, 'it's not half as tasteless as coming as an Australian.'

Ronnie Corbett stood up at a dinner held to celebrate what was affectionately known as Bruce Forsyth's hundred years in show business. 'I remember seeing Bruce in *Cinderella*,' said Ronnie. 'He was on the stage with Cinders and she said, "Oh, Buttons, I'm so unhappy. I wish there was someone here who could sing and dance and tell jokes."' Ronnie waited. Then he said, 'The next time we saw her, we'd forgotten who she was.'

Spike Mullins (see earlier) wrote that. Spike, Ronnie and Bruce all in one story. A bumper bundle.

Two singer-actresses, Barry Humphries (in full drag as Dame Edna) and I stood in the wings at the Palladium during the finale of a charity show. We had all been on and done our various acts.

'I was crap,' said the first singer-actress, 'and two people have told me I was brilliant.'

'I was absolute b* * * * * *s,' said the second singer-actress, 'and three people said I was great. The secret is that inside we know we're crap, but we can enjoy the praise as well.'

Dame Edna leant in. 'If we held ourselves in high esteem,' said Barry, 'we wouldn't even be doing this.'

Mike Yarwood told me that, on the day that John Kennedy was assassinated, there was to be boxing televised from Birmingham town hall. It was, of course, cancelled. His father, a keen fan of pugilistic art, was disappointed, but kept a tactful silence. The next day, he said to Mike, 'I'm sorry, but sometimes I wish he'd never been killed.'

I sat with Bud Flanagan in the last year of his life, at

rehearsals for a show called *Stars and Garters*. He was at the end of a long career. 'Are you Jewish, son?' he asked me.

'No,' I said.

'Don't worry,' he said, 'it doesn't show.'

He must have sung his theme songs 'Underneath the Arches' and 'Strolling' hundreds of times. I asked him if he ever got tired of them and bored with the endless repetition. 'Of course,' he said, 'but I run a shop and, if the customers come in and I haven't got what they want, I'm out of business.' I couldn't have put it better myself. That's why I quoted him.

When I was a young comic, I would sometimes make smart-arsed remarks about the smallness of the audience. An older performer took me to one side. 'Never make fun of them,' he said, 'they're the ones who have come to see you.'

Willie Rushton's favourite pieces of advice were: first, never go to a dentist with blood in his hair; and, secondly, never holiday in a country where they still point at planes. To which I add: never go to a doctor who has dying plants in his waiting room.

The scene was Vienna. I was with Victor Kiam, the man who liked his razor so much, he bought the company. The air-traffic controllers' strike was in progress and we were stuck. The night before, we had spoken at a dinner and we were debating how to spend our unexpected extra day. Victor had expressed a desire to visit Yugoslavia for the afternoon, but he was dissuaded. The considered verdict was that we might well get in, but probably wouldn't get out.

He had been a young GI at the end of the Second World War in Vienna and he took me round some of his old haunts; it was all evocative of *The Third Man*. He was the most stimulating company imaginable. The famous Ferris wheel, where Orson Welles delivered the 'cuckoo clock' speech, was closed, but apart from that it was a memorable day.

He told me that he once thought of taking over a lingerie company. He sat in a boardroom with the directors. He noticed that men seldom knew bra sizes when buying for their partners and suggested giving the cup sizes names, instead of letters and numbers. His proposed idea for the four main sizes was: Ping Pong, Ding Dong, Hong Kong, and Holy Cow! This was greeted with silence. He went back to his first love, razors.

My long-time partner, Dick Vosburgh, was on tour with a Bruce Forsyth vehicle, *The Travelling Music Show*. When I say 'vehicle', it was definitely in need of servicing and Dick was virtually writing it as they went along. Not a perfect situation. The good news was that he was in the company of Burt Shevelove, a Broadway veteran and co-author of *A Funny Thing Happened on the Way to the Forum*. One night, Dick and Burt went to a restaurant that Burt had already visited.

'Order pasta,' said Burt.

Dick demurred; he felt like a steak.

'Just for me, order pasta,' persisted Burt.

Dick reluctantly agreed.

After the food arrived, a waitress approached. 'Palmerston cheese?' she asked. Dick kept a straight face and accepted.

As she left, Burt leant over. 'Now you know why I wanted you to order the pasta,' he said.

Dick sat with Burt, watching auditions for the show. A tenor sang on stage. Burt was huddled in an overcoat. He was old and ill. He turned to Dick and said, 'This guy sings like I feel.'

Dick was once at a party chez Cryer. Our daughter, Jacqui, was at the crawling stage. As she made her way across the floor, someone trod on her. I picked her up and comforted her. Dick loomed out of the crowd. 'Tell me who did it and I'll write for them,' he said.

I once asked his opinion of a certain actress. 'A diamond wouldn't make an impression on the softest part of her,' was his response.

Trini Lopez, who had a lot of success with his band in the States, became a film actor briefly and visited England to appear in the film *The Dirty Dozen*. While he was here, he was signed to host a TV show. Dick and I were deputed to go and see him at the Carlton Towers Hotel. He was in the company of his manager, 'Bullets' Durgan, a Runyonesque character with a 'colourful' background. The show was called *Hippo-drome* and was set in a circus ring. It was fronted by a star, host and ringmaster, in this case Trini. Our producer began to sell the show to him. He was clearly exhausted after a long day's filming. The producer enthused over the ambience of the settings, the ring, the real lions in real cages, the elephants, the clowns, the beautiful trapeze artists . . . On and on he went. He suggested, in a rare burst of creativity, that Trini could describe how, as a little boy, he had run away from home to the big top and lifted the flap to gaze at the wonders therein. He finished his sales pitch. He was now exhausted.

'I hate f* * * * *g circuses,' said Trini.

Dick, in years gone by, was possessed of a flowing mane of hair and a wild beard. On a programme called *Whose Baby*, where the panel had to guess famous fathers and mothers, he sat behind a screen while his six children answered questions.

'Who looks most like your father?' said the host.

'Rasputin,' said one of his daughters.

Ah, the genes have it.

Graham Weatherell was the producer of *3-2-1* on Yorkshire television. The programme had a penchant for guest stars of the fifties and sixties vintage. They were nostalgic and they were cheaper. Guy Mitchell, a big star in the fifties, was touring England. He was booked to appear on the show. Graham received a message that Mr Mitchell had arrived at the reception. He hurried to greet the star. He rushed forward, extending his hand. Guy Mitchell, too, thrust out his hand. As he did so, his shoulder bag slid down his arm and fell to the floor. They both bent to pick it up. Their heads clashed. Guy's teeth fell out on the floor and broke. Where do you find a dental mechanic on a Sunday in Leeds? You couldn't write it. But then again, I just did.

I've already mentioned Arthur Askey in connection with *Joker's Wild*. I worked with him on other shows, including his last TV appearance, and we had become friends. Sadly, he developed gangrene and had his leg amputated. I visited him in St Thomas's Hospital. Ever ebullient, he greeted me. He showed me a telegram he had received from an old friend. It read: 'Have got you the part of Long John Silver in the tour of *Treasure Island*' Arthur was much amused. Tragically, his condition worsened and he lost his other leg. I went to see him again, desperately putting on a cheerful face. I entered his room. He lay in bed. The sheets were heart-breakingly flat. And he was laughing and said, 'You remember that man who sent me the telegram?' I did. 'He's sent me another one,' he said, and showed it to me. It said: 'Calm down, you've got the job.'

Dickie Henderson came to see him around the same time. They watched the news. The old ship, the *Mary Rose*, was being lifted from the depths, where it had lain for centuries. 'What a relief,' said Arthur, 'my band parts are on that.'

A load of City fat cats were having a river trip on the Thames, during which they would pass St Thomas's Hospital. They asked if Arthur could be wheeled out on to the balcony so they could greet him by loud hailer. The message came back that Mr Askey would be delighted but after his ordeal he would be too weak to do more than shout his catch phrase, 'Hello, playmates!', through the hospital's sound system. The boat came to a halt in the middle of the river opposite the hospital. Sure enough, there was Arthur on the balcony. A roar of greeting went up from the boat. 'Hello, playmates!' called Arthur. He then did 35 minutes. Small of stature, he was one of the biggest men I ever knew.

Dickie Henderson, with his husky, mid-Atlantic voice, never failed to make me laugh. I sat with him at a lunch and during the meal someone came up and asked him to introduce the cabaret, as they had been let down at the last minute. Ever cooperative, he agreed and then pulled a face at me. He was introduced on to the stage. As he began to speak, four men clumped on behind him and began, noisily, to set up four heavy stand mikes. Dickie battled on. After a couple of minutes of this, he turned and looked at them and the mikes. He turned back to the audience and said, 'I wouldn't mind, but it's a dog act.'

I once went to a charity lunch at the Intercontinental Hotel in London. (The two constant themes of this book seem to be pubs and charity. Perhaps my real vocation is the Salvation Army.) There was, as usual, a raffle. I won first prize. I was astonished and, for some reason, guilty. I'd bought tickets, but I was a guest. The first prize was a beautiful set of pewter. I gave a lordly wave and asked them to draw again. Applause – what a nice man. Afterwards, Dickie came up to me.

'Never do that,' he said.

'Why?' I asked.

'Screws it for the rest of us,' he replied.

While in self-congratulatory mode – will that OBE never come? – I agreed to open a garden party for DISC (Disability in Camden) some years ago. In the interim, I tore a ligament while playing tennis with one of our sons. Came the day of the fête and I was on elbow crutches. As we drove there, my wife started to laugh.

'Have you seen what you look like?' she said.

I realised I was going into a garden full of wheelchairs.

We arrived and I hobbled over to a chair and was offered a cup of tea. A girl in a wheelchair came bowling over to me. 'I think you people are wonderful,' she said. 'Do you do all your own housework?'

The humour of the handicapped never ceases to delight me. I pushed over a pile of pennies at a pub in Harrow, in aid of Guide Dogs for the Blind. The organiser said that a man in the corner with his dog wanted to say hello. I went over. 'Hello, Jack, it's Barry,' I said. We chatted.

'Someone told me you are always on the Metropolitan Line from Harrow on the Hill,' he said.

I confirmed that it was so nearly every day.

'So am I,' said Jack.

'I've never seen you there,' I said.

'I've never seen *you* there,' he replied.

I was told this joke by a blind man. There was a blind parachutist who did jumps for charity. Someone asked him how he knew when he was getting near the ground. 'The lead on my guide dog goes slack,' he said.

The acquiring of white hair, coupled with advancing years, leads to the illusion of vast wisdom and experience, which I exploit to the hilt. But when it's truly deserved, as in the case of director Billy Wilder, it can lead to superb lines. After a long glittering Hollywood career, he was still trying to set up projects with young producers. The story goes that he was sitting in an office with a young tycoon, who said, 'Mr Wilder, would you mind telling me what you've done?'

'A fair question,' said the maestro. 'You go first.'

A veteran actress, Athene Seyler, when asked at an interview what she had done, replied, 'You mean this morning?'

A friend of mine referred to a young producer as a 'sperm in a suit'. Lines like that just get recycled. When the former Tory leader William Hague's name was mentioned, Joan Collins said, 'Darling, he looks like a foetus.' *Plus ça change* . . .

The ego is a delicate blossom which is forever being punctured. All right, you can't puncture a blossom, but you know what I mean. Anyway, any illusion that people in our profession float on some pink cloud of unawareness must be firmly dispelled. Brutal reality is always intruding.

We were filming with Kenny Everett outside the aforementioned St Thomas's Hospital when one of the hospital employees approached me and said, 'Give us your autograph, Bal.'

'Certainly,' I said.

'You didn't think I was serious?' he quipped.

Some weeks later, I was in a taxi going over, or rather across, Westminster Bridge – 'over' sounds a little dramatic. I don't think I've recovered from the punctured blossom yet. The driver and I were chatting away and I told him the story of the man who said, 'You didn't think I was serious?'

He laughed heartily and then said, 'Imagine that happening to someone well known!'

Dawn French and Jennifer Saunders tell the story of giving their autographs to two women at an airport. After assuring them how much they enjoyed their work, the women moved away. As they did so, Dawn and Jennifer heard one say, after looking at the signatures, 'Still none the wiser.'

Michael Parkinson was sitting in a Manchester store at a book-signing session. Two women stood close by. Finally, after studying him closely, one said to the other, 'He doesn't take daylight, does he?'

John Junkin was in a pub and noticed a couple staring at him. As he said himself, he preened himself and checked in his pockets to see if he had a pen handy. The man came over. 'Do you drive a lorry?' he asked.

'No,' said John.

'You've got a bloody double,' said the man.

The unstoppable Frank Carson was asked by a woman for his autograph in Dublin. She informed him that it was for her daughter and produced a crumpled cigarette packet.

Frank duly signed. The woman looked and said, 'Ah, that's grand. I'll copy it into her book when I get home.'

My friend Joyce Howard, sister-in-law of Frankie Vaughan, was doing cabaret on the *QE2*. I know the situation well. You have a captive audience and you are their captive performer. You are liable to meet them the next day. As she strolled on the deck, a man introduced himself and told her how much he'd enjoyed her performance the night before. She thanked him. He said, 'When you sang "I left My Heart in San Francisco", you *looked* like Tony Bennett.'

To sum up this saga of scrambled egos, my first employer, David Nixon, told me a story of the early days of *What's My Line?* on BBC television. One of his fellow panellists was Gilbert Harding, an irascible, gifted man with a huge reputation. They came out of the stage door one night to be confronted by a crowd of autograph hunters. As Gilbert fumbled in his pocket, he heard someone say, 'You'd think he'd have a pen.'

The next week, he said to David, 'I'm prepared,' and took out a pen.

They went out through the door and a voice said, 'Look at him with his pen out!'

The last word. Hermione Gingold, a great revue star, came out of a stage door on Broadway and heard a small boy say to his father, 'What's that lady *for*?'

To which there is no answer.

THIRTY-THREE

UNDER THE INFLUENCE

EVERYONE, EVEN Adolf Hitler, Saddam Hussein or Chris Evans, must admit to people who have influenced and inspired them. Role models are an essential part of life, representing, as they do, something to aspire to and learn from. Very early on, I knew that my mother had certain amazing qualities that I admired. One was a two-sided coin: her endless imperturbability which could irritate me but also proved a source of strength. Widowed, with two sons to bring up, she calmly got on with it. This is not to say that she had no temper. Her infrequent explosions were impressive, precisely because they seemed out of character. She epitomised what I was saying about Ayckbourn characters who lead their lives in quiet, relentless sequence, until a snapping point occurs.

When I finally got to university, I knew she was proud, but little was said. 'Very nice' was an emotional outburst in her vocabulary. When I fell from grace, there was no recrimination, no rebuke, just a clear indication that I would be supported, whatever I chose to do next. The other side of the coin.

Her fastidious attention to detail made it even more painful when, towards the end of her life, confusion set in. She used to pop into the local Chinese restaurant for a cup of tea and they would ring to tell us that she was there. One winter's afternoon, she emerged from the restaurant into darkness before we got there and was frightened by the gloom. Her health deteriorated and we reluctantly entrusted her to the care of a local home, as she was in need of constant medical care. On our visits, I noticed the puzzlement with which she greeted me. I was bearded and this obviously bewildered her. She was always aware that my wife was her daughter-in-law, but who was this man with her? The situation became even more complicated when she greeted our eldest son. Tony, as 'Barry'. She had slipped a generation – her son was a boy. The sadness was not without its humour. She was once discovered attacking her colostomy bag with a pair of scissors and, on one occasion, threw it across the room and nearly went with it. I plead guilty to finding that funny: you need some smiles at times like that. Billy Connolly has been criticised for finding some aspects of his father's Alzheimer's funny. He is entitled to do so and, equally, other people are allowed their reaction to his stories. When my mother died, a major prop in my life had gone. As I told you, I never really knew my father.

But I now had the rock of my life, my wife. We met under bizarre circumstances, with me bandaged and concealed behind dark glasses, but things improved and have done for 47 years to date. When you are often away from home, it's great to know that the nest is still there to fly back to and my wife's support has been constant. This is exemplified in the way that she sits, smiling and laughing at my side, when I'm speaking at some function or other. She has heard most of the jokes before, but it doesn't show. What an actress. Her knowledge of our business has been an enormous help, and proves, if proof were needed, that a partner who actually knows what you're doing when you're at work is a definite asset.

Four children arrived over some ten years and they, too, have shown a degree of understanding and patience that I'm grateful for. In case you think I'm trying to paint some idyllic picture of the ideal family, this is not so. We've had many ups and downs – with four children, you are certainly increasing the odds – but I think we've all survived.

The roll of honour of influences part two. Horace Bradbrook, our English master at school, who instilled in me a feeling that drama was exciting and not something just to be endured. The benign Pip Kelsey; I have already mentioned his painfully accurate comment on my last school report. Johnny Gunn, the stage manager at the Empire Theatre in Leeds (I'm sure you could hardly forget). He convinced me that maybe I could actually take the game up professionally and embarked on teaching me. Jimmy Gay, a comedian who was always on the verge of being discovered. He came to Leeds with a touring revue and I was immediately impressed. The repose and the timing betokened years of experience. One immaculately incorrect sketch in which he appeared involved his unwittingly eating catfood in an ethnic restaurant. It was memorable only for his exquisite portrayal of a man turning into a cat.

This was during my period of working as a stagehand and he invited me into his dressing room. I wearily entered, as I had already had one uneasy incident with a comic in the same dressing room, which I shall not go into here as it was, firstly, fleeting, secondly, tawdry, and, thirdly, this is not a kiss and tell exercise. My amazing and tempestuous love life must wait for another volume, or, more likely, I'll turn the volume down.

Meanwhile, back in the room with Jimmy Gay (his surname had no significance, I assure you), he poured me a Guinness and told me he had heard that I wanted to go into show business. He then embarked on a lecture, delineating each and every reason why this was not a good idea. He finished, looked at me, and said, 'People used to say all this to me and I never took any bloody notice. Have another Guinness.'

I still remember the line in his act when he told the audience that at the Apothecary's Hall, Normanton, business was so bad that one night somebody shot a stag in the gallery. The Apothecary's Hall, Normanton – such colourful detail is, to me, the mark of a real comedian.

That tradition continued with Les Dawson. Les once

announced that he had another engagement: he was due to appear at a Mafia hotpot supper. Sheer joy.

Jimmy Gay continued touring the country and never got the big break. Towards the end of his life, he succumbed to mental decline and was resident in a hospital outside Leeds. Barney Colehan, the TV producer, yet another great influence in my life, met Jimmy when he (Barney) took an amateur operatic company of which he was president to entertain the patients at this hospital. He noticed a suave figure, in a brocade dressing gown, smoking through a long holder at the back of the audience. Not a displaced Noël Coward, but Jimmy Gay. The performance, which, by Barney's account, was long and well meaning but a severe test of the patients' patience, had finished and Barney went over to speak to Jimmy. Jimmy remembered him and, nodding towards the cast, said, 'Is this part of the treatment?'

The 'nearly, but not quite' breed of comedians, who had everything except the killer instinct required to make the final lap, always endeared themselves to me. Jimmy Edmundson and Johnny Silver at the Windmill, who could entertain a sparse house that had come to see the girls, but never let it affect their endless flow of invention and good humour, were two classic examples.

Leslie Crowther, who achieved a great measure of TV fame, was fascinating on the subject of the qualities of a great comedian. Modest as ever, he once said to me, 'I'm not a great comedian, but I'm a good one.'

'You're great man, Les,' I riposted.

'Marry me,' he said.

Les once forgot the words of a song at a Royal Variety performance, transmitted live to millions of viewers. He stopped the orchestra, beamed at the audience and said, 'I'm so glad this is live – now you can see the sort of thing that really happens.' And then he started the song again.

Influences, influences. Vivian Van Damm, my boss at the Windmill, who never lost faith in me when all around him were telling him he was wrong.

Charles Ross, who signed me, a relatively inexperienced writer, to write the major part of a revue, single-handed. I wasn't ready then and I couldn't do it now, but of course I loved him for it. The show was called *See You Inside* – imagine what the critics made of that. The support of Jon Pertwee, who stood firm through all the travails of a flop. An object-lesson in loyalty.

Danny La Rue, who entrusted the writing of his nightclub shows to me year in and year out and taught me to face an audience head on, at very short range.

David Frost, who not only took me on as a writer but threw me into the deep end as a warm-up man, which stood me in good stead for several years, when the writing became thin on the ground.

Peter Vincent, my old friend, who taught me the value of sheer slog, whereas I've always been inclined to cut corners.

Dick Vosburgh, for just being funny, patient and fast.

The many hours spent writing with him were some of the happiest ever.

Maurice Browning and Denis Martin at the Players' Theatre, my joint mentors, who introduced me to the joys of being a music-hall chairman and host – the human Polyfiller that hopefully holds the show together.

And John Dowie, the loving bully who browbeat me into dispensing with any memory aids on stage when I first did my so-called one-man show (with Colin Sell at the piano). I had what I considered an artfully concealed book with large subject headings on a music stand by the piano. I would frequently gaze at it to remind myself where I had got to.

'Get rid of that f* * * * *g book,' said John. 'This show started in your head – get it back in there.'

The first night I discarded the crutch was at the Brighton Festival, when I went out and just began to talk, as opposed to sneaking looks at the book. The legendary Joan Littlewood was in the audience with Victor Spinetti. I met her afterwards.

'I heard about the book,' she said. 'I always said you were an amateur.'

You need these people.

Jim Moir, former head of Light Entertainment, BBC television, who became the boss of Radio 2, whose unfailing good humour and all-embracing knowledge of his territory made me realise later that I was being taught without knowing it. One of his wise words, commenting on comedians who tried to ad lib before they had actually mastered the script, was, 'You can't play the jazz until you've learnt the music.' He produced *The Generation Game* with Bruce Forsyth and, during rehearsals, would regale us with a wickedly accurate impression of Bruce, when the maestro was not there. He also produced Mike Yarwood's show and taught Mike the Bruce impression. Jim's endless amiability coped with quite a few barbs, including one at his retirement party. Jim is, shall we say, comfortably built, and Mike referred to him as 'a man who can light up a room just by moving away from the window'. His approach to his work – taking it seriously, but never himself – has stayed with me. He had a habit of describing the process of writing as 'cobbling the script together'. One day, he entered an office and, spotting Spike Mullins (ibid.) and I sitting in the corner, sprang back in mock alarm. 'Writers!' he cried. 'Cobblers,' Spike and I replied in unison.

The first time I met Spike was at the initial meeting for *The Two Ronnies*. I had heard of this man who wrote for Max Bygraves and had been co-opted into the team. Immaculate in a safari suit, with neat white beard and glasses, he sat alone. I approached and introduced myself. We chatted and I asked him where he lived. He said Farnham Royal, outside Slough, and that it had taken an hour and three quarters to get to the meeting. 'A long time without a woman,' he observed.

He is still sorely missed by the writing mafia. He was one of the few writers I know – Dick Vosburgh is another

– who is regularly quoted by their peers. At Spike's funeral, his friend, Peter Robinson, commented that it was amazing that Spike had turned up, as he hated funerals.

My contention that there is no real generation gap in comedy also holds for those you respect. Richard Curtis, co-author of *Blackadder*, writer of *Four Weddings and a Funeral*, *The Vicar of Dibley* and other jewels in our crown, was a driving force in the first Comic Relief. Very soon, I learnt to respect his quiet, self-effacing authority. You know it when it's there. If he said something, you listened. And, of course, his talent has been amply proven.

Richard rang me once, just after my wife and I had left home to go to Buckingham Palace. (I can placedrop, too.) Our eldest son suggested that Richard should ring me there in 45 minutes. As we entered the hallowed precincts, a flunkey approached and said, 'Mr Cryer, there's a call for you.' This was overheard by several people and I was mortified. That is a lie: I was delighted.

On the night of the first Comic Relief Red Nose extra-vaganza, I was deputed by Richard to be a 'greeter', i.e. when artists arrived I was to go down to reception, welcome them and settle them in. While waiting for someone, I saw Jim Davidson and Ben Elton hovering. I couldn't resist the opportunity to introduce these two inhabitants of rather different planets. They chatted and Ben asked Jim if he was staying all night.

'No,' said Jim, 'I've got a National Front meeting at nine.'

Ben went round quoting this line delightedly.

The joyful mix continued when Cannon and Ball arrived from their pantomime at the Palladium. I duly took them upstairs and Bobby Ball caught sight of Ade Edmundson. Ade, offstage, is quiet (well, quieter), bespectacled and far removed from the demented punk we know and love. I introduced them and they chatted about slapstick. I suppose I'm a practising catalyst.

Writers, as I've said before, are normally tolerant, magnanimous creatures and the revered heavyweights of our profession, like Galton, Simpson and Johnny Speight, are ever interested in new developments in comedy. Alan Simpson and Ray Galton, in particular, not only agreed to help our youngest son with a thesis but invited him over for tea. I introduced two young tyro writers to Johnny Speight and he treated them as equals. I thank all of those three gentle knights again.

Talking of tolerance, I remember with affection Father Kieron at the Dominican Priory in Chalk Farm, who gave me 'instruction' when I was about to be married. In those days (circa 1962), any pagan marrying a Catholic was required to go through a process of instruction. I was intrigued. Father K and I would sit and chat, drinking Benedictine – as opposed to Dominican – and would finally get round to the subject in hand. The relevance of this is that he reassured me that he had no intention of trying to convert me, averring that he had scared off more than he had won over.

Our friendship grew and one day he asked me if I knew Albert Finney. Throwing caution to the winds, I said that I did. It was strictly true, as I had met Albert in 1958 when I was in *Expresso Bongo* and he was making his first appearance in London in *The Party* with Charles Laughton. But I hadn't seen him since. Father K's interest in Albert sprang from the fact that he was appearing in John Osborne's play *Luther* (Albert Finney, not Father Kieron. Now, that *would* have been a casting coup). The monks at the priory were fascinated by the play, dealing as it did with the arch iconoclast, and several of them had been given dispensation to unfrock themselves and sally forth to see the play. I was committed to contacting my famous friend.

I rang the stage door at the Phoenix Theatre and asked if he was around. 'He's just walked in,' said the doorkeeper. Father K had asked me to invite him to lunch. I took a deep breath and prepared to start the laborious process of reminding Albert who I was. I needn't have bothered. He remembered our previous meeting, relaxing me immediately, and readily accepted the invitation. I got married in the interim. (Actually in St John's in Bristol.)

Come the day of the lunch, I was submerged in flu but determined to turn up. The doorbell rang, and there stood Albert with a bandaged arm. I think he had fallen off a horse while filming *Tom Jones*. We made a sorry pair. We made our way to the priory. The whole occasion was a great success. Once a month, the monks, who were a silent order, had a vocal lunch, and this was it. During the meal, we had a reading from *Lady Chatterley's Lover*. I am not making this up.

I still bump into Albert from time to time and neither of us has forgotten that day, but then you wouldn't, would you? Just as I have never forgotten the day I fell off Tom Jones while filming a horse, but that's another story.

My father-in-law, Teddy, bore a strange resemblance to Spencer Tracy and made a very strong impression on me. I did the traditional thing and asked him for his daughter's hand in marriage. This was as we walked across the Clifton suspension bridge. He gave his blessing and then suggested we both jump off. This was my introduction to the Donovan clan and allied branches. For someone who had a rather solitary childhood, this was an overwhelming experience, and I still recall being driven round Brighton and its environs one Sunday in a frantic succession of meetings with uncles and aunties. To be embraced into such a hierarchy has been a source of some joy and not a little bewilderment. Let's just say, they've taught me all about what the playwright Dodie Smith called *Dear Octopus* – long may the family tentacles cling.

Willie Rushton once observed that he had had enough of erratic geniuses and temperamental prima donnas and that all he wanted from life was to be with people he liked and laugh a lot. I'll drink to that.

Which brings me to Denis King. I met the King brothers

in the late fifties. They had established themselves as a top act in the dear, dead days of dinner jackets and Brylcreem and soon became valued friends. Denis and I subsequently worked together for years in radio on the programme *Hello Cheeky* and he went on to become an established composer, both of musicals and music for television series. His influence on me has been one of sheer good nature. Whatever his problems, they are not shared. His priority is your company and the job in hand. Never take someone like that for granted. They should be available on prescription.

In the fifties, as I've mentioned, I was plagued by ill health. One Christmas Day, I found myself in hospital. It wasn't difficult – I was in the bed in the corner. On the day, the ward was buzzing with activity and bedecked with bunting. Friends and families were visiting, carols were playing through a speaker and all was festivity. I had no visitors, being away from home and having been admitted at such short notice that nobody knew I was there. I read a book and pretended to sleep.

I was woken by the sensation that I was not alone. I opened my eyes and peered through the slits in my bandages. This was during my invisible-man period, in which I was swathed from head to foot. There stood the three King brothers, their mother, father and sister, Moira. They told me some story about hearing that I was in there and as they were passing . . . They gave my presents, talked and laughed, and then they left. They had rescued my Christmas Day from self-pitying misery. On Boxing Day, they came *again*. Excuse me, I have to attend to this lump in my throat.

Mention of the King brothers reminds me that we were all working under the aegis of Paul Cave, Frankie Vaughan's manager, my mentor and friend. Hard to imagine now, but Frank was the Beatles of his day. I once sat in a car with him that was unable to move due to the crowds that besieged it outside the Hammersmith Palais. All I could see were flushed faces pressed against the windows. Through the windscreen, I could see bodies draped on the bonnet. The noise was deafening and the car was rocking. It was alarming and exhilarating. We finally drove off slowly and carefully, shepherded by the police. Lonnie Donegan was a similar phenomenon in the fifties. Queues round the block of, yes, the Empire Theatre, Leeds. The frenzy induced by skiffle, which, in real terms, only lasted some three years, is hard to imagine today.

(*Note for young readers: 'skiffle' was pastiche American folk music, performed by groups and consisting of guitars, a bass made from a tea chest and a broom handle and sometimes a washboard, played with thimbles on the fingers. Once again, I am not making this up.)

Why should certain performers provoke such a reaction? Now, the brothers Gallagher can produce a similar effect. The fact that they strike me as ersatz Beatles is neither here nor there – as the man said when he put his truss on upside down. (If a joke's worth doing once, it's worth doing twice!)

Incidentally, that was a joke from my act in the fifties that I've just remembered. It's a miracle I'm still here.

Rostropovich, the great cellist, was recording with an orchestra in the middle of the afternoon when he threw a tantrum and walked out. The manager of the studio was informed; he rushed down in the lift and confronted Rostropovich in the lobby: 'I believe you are not satisfied with my studio,' he said.

Rostropovich agreed and then proceeded, at some length, to tell him why.

When he paused for breath, the manager said, 'For your information, I've had thirty years' experience running a studio.'

'I think not,' said the great man. 'I think you've had one year's experience, thirty times.'

How true.

I must go – I'm just starting my first year's experience for the seventy-fourth time. See you there.

ACKNOWLEDGEMENTS

MANY THANKS TO Steve Knight and Mike Whitehill, whose patience and enthusiasm helped to get this project off the ground and Emma Darrell, whose discipline and organisational skills helped to make sure that the book was finally finished.